The Train Keeps Leaving *Without Me*

The Train Keeps Leaving *Without Me*

A PRACTICAL GUIDE TO HAPPINESS, FREEDOM, & SELF-FULFILLMENT

Dr. Michael Osit

Special discounts in bulk quantities are available to corporations, professional associations and other organizations.

For details contact:
Dr. Michael Osit
5 Mountain Boulevard
Suite 4
Warren, NJ 07059
Tel: 908.757.1399x2
E-mail: Dr.Michael.Osit@Gmail.Com
Website: WWW.WPAAPC.Com

This publication is intended to provide accurate and authoritative information in regard to the subject matter. It is sold with the understanding that the contents can be helpful to individuals but not all individuals. It is not meant to replace psychotherapy or treatment for any psychological or mental illness. Individuals should seek appropriate treatment from a licensed professional when indicated.

To Terri, Daniel, Marilyn, Nicole, Matt,
Matthew & Amanda,

The joy you give me is enough for a lifetime of
happiness, freedom, and self-fulfillment

Contents

PART ONE
The Basics

CHAPTER 1

Life Doesn't Have To Be So Terrible

If You Do Something About it

The Train Keeps Leaving Without Me!

I was sitting across from a 20-year-old patient. Charlie has been a patient of mine, now in college, commuting by train to take his classes. He angrily informs me that his professor for his Monday morning History class is threatening to fail him.

"*What do you think the problem is in that class for you?*" I ask.

Charlie looks down at his $200 Nike LeBron XII sneakers and sheepishly says, "*I have too many absences.*"

"*What is getting in the way of you attending this Monday morning class?*"

Charlie looks up at me, leans forward, and answers my question, in a not so sheepish tone of voice.

"*Dr. Osit, he asserts, it's not my fault. The train keeps leaving without me! And besides, he adds, this class is not that big of a deal anyway.*"

The train keeps leaving without him. Oh! That is why he can't make his class and is in danger of failing. And let's not forget. Charlie also told me "his professor" is threatening to fail him. Poor Charlie. Both the professor and New Jersey Transit are causing him so much difficulty in this class.

This little vignette is rich in life lessons. The most obvious is Charlie's lack of ownership and responsibility for his misfortune. Charlie actually displaces blame on everyone else except himself. I am surprised Charlie didn't add the fact that he kept missing his train was because the hands on his watch kept going past the time the train was too far from the train station. Charlie's perspective is that he is a victim in this situation. Also, Charlie is not actually doing anything about resolving his Monday morning class problem, he is simply complaining about it. And then, he dismisses the problem by devaluing its importance. What will change if he maintains this faulty thinking? He rationalizes, justifies, and has, what he believes, is a great excuse. Missing the train was just the beginning of Charlie's unhappiness. He ran his life this way. His relationships with family and friends were either contentious and, at times, completely nonexistent. He was mildly successful in some of his classes, but encountered performance issues in others, and at his part-time job as well. He was late with assignments, did them last minute, lost interest in his major, and experienced a great deal of stress in his life. Charlie had some positive attributes. In fact, Charlie had many positive traits. However, they were mostly overshadowed due to the way he was running his life. People, as well as himself, would only see glimpses of how he positively contributed to his relationships. In turn, Charlie was not living the quality of life he so wanted to have. He felt stagnant, trapped and helpless.

Now, as an outsider looking in (at this actual true story) it may seem rather obvious to you how ridiculous Charlie's, thinking is regarding his situation. But, it is highly possible, that in some ways, you may be less than happy in your life due to your thinking that a train is leaving without you. It may not be as obvious to you, and it may not be as extreme as Charlie's story, but, you may believe that there are a bunch of trains in your life that are leaving without you. This book is about taking control and accepting full responsibility in your life and for your life. It is about taking control over what you can take control over so that the train doesn't leave without you. It is a guide to living a happy, free, and self-fulfilled life.

Do Something About It

Reading this book is a great step toward taking control of your life and opening doors to great things for yourself. If you are going to simply read this book and not try to integrate my suggestions into your life, then please, stop reading now. What I have to tell you is far too important to merely put this book down after the final page is read and think that what I have to say is extremely interesting and very relatable to your life. I sit with countless patients who simply complain about their lives, thank me for my great suggestions to make positive changes, yet do absolutely nothing about it-week after week-session after session. Of course, I call them out on their inertia and eventually they either make changes for the better, drop out of therapy, or I ask them to leave and return when they are ready to work-really work. Admittedly, many of the ideas you will read about are common sense-maybe even simplistic. Sometimes it is extremely helpful to review the basics just to be sure you are standing on firm ground. No matter who you are, what you do for a living or how much money you make, the pragmatic concepts offered throughout this book need to be implemented in your life, in your way, if you want to approach happiness, freedom, and self-fulfillment. So, are you willing to not only think about my ideas but are you actually willing to apply them to yourself and how you are conducting your life? If the answer to this question is *"yes"* then you are on your way to leading the life you can have-not just the life you wish for. But Lesson One is to be careful. Make sure what I say makes sense and applies to you. I am confident it will, but I still want you to scrutinize my ideas and apply them to the way you live your life.

The Bad News

I know nothing about you. I have never met you. I don't know your history, your trials and tribulations, the quality of your present relationships, or what has happened in your past relationships. I don't know your passions, your likes and dislikes, or the kind of music you like to listen to. I don't know if you are gay or straight, are in a romantic relationship, or even have friends. I don't know your personality traits, your thought process, or how you cope with difficulties in your life. I don't know your intimate thoughts and feelings, or even if you are aware of them.

Since I don't know you, I can't know your strengths and weaknesses. I don't know your past transgressions and the accumulation of experiences and feelings you have from your past and present. It is your job to know and understand yourself. I trust that you will read these pages with an open mind while keeping your defenses at bay.

The Good News

But, in a way, I do know you and you will come to realize this as you pass through these pages. We haven't met, but there are ideas I present that will strike a chord within you. How do I know this? Am I pretentious enough to suggest that you are just like everyone else in the world? That you are not unique or different enough to be interesting and intriguing? That we are all similar enough for me to make generalizations about our personalities and the way we live our lives?

It is crystal clear to me that everyone has their own unique process during their lifespan. Sure, we all have some similarities but each of us experiences life in our own way, through our own looking glass. You have to try to make sense out of your interactions within yourself as well as with the world around you so that it works for you. My hope is that what I have to tell you is helpful and you will be able to apply it in a way that is satisfying and beneficial.

Who Am I, To Tell You?

In my work as a Psychologist, I have had the privilege of entering the lives of thousands of patients over the past forty years. The therapeutic relationship is unlike any other relationship in the world. Just think about it. A stranger is meeting another stranger, with no history together. Immediately, the patient is expected to reveal their inner most feelings, secrets and problems. It is unnatural and sort of strange, but that is the expectation of both me and the patient sitting across from me. Here is a perfect example. A 36-year-old woman is attending her first session with me. She sits down, shuffles her body in the chair a bit as she settles in. I ask her how I can help her. She immediately replies, "Well, I'm having an affair with my husband's male lover but my husband doesn't know about it." Now, you probably had to read that line twice but it is exactly what she told me. This is not the type of information you would tell a person that you only met two minutes ago. The assumption is, in a therapeutic relationship, that the most fundamental and integral aspect is that there is 100% trust and confidentiality. And that is just the beginning. As the therapeutic alliance progresses, the patient talks to the therapist as if he or she were speaking into a mirror. The fact that it is another person they are revealing their most intimate thoughts, feelings, and experiences is almost irrelevant. When a patient lies to me I tell them that they haven't lied to me-only to themselves.

It is a one-way relationship. It is never about me, my feelings, my thoughts, my values, my judgments. It is pure and direct in terms of the goal of the relationship. That goal is to help the person sitting across from me to be happy by modifying or sometimes dramatically changing how they are conducting their lives and their relationships. The intimacy, trust, and therapeutic alliance creates the most unique relationship on the planet. It enables me to get to know people in a way that no one else in their life does, and it is a one-way relationship where they only need to attend to their own thoughts, feelings and behavior without considering the effect on me. It is pure, with no outside influences, enabling the patient to grow in the ultimate sense of the word.

Lourdes, a woman who has been cleaning my house on a weekly basis for 25 years was leaving to visit family in Portugal for a month. Being the responsible individual she is, she arranged to have a friend of hers take her place in her absence. One Friday morning, Lourdes brought her friend with her to show her how she goes about doing her job. I caught glimpses of Lourdes instructing Maria on all of the basics and nuances of cleaning the Osit household. She knew every inch of my home, and was able to convey to Maria the best, most efficient way of getting each job done. Lourdes knew all of the nuances, where to streamline and where not to cut corners. It was apparent to me, although not surprising, that Lourdes had accumulated a tremendous amount of knowledge about her job over the past 25 years.

Like Lourdes and anyone else who, for decades, puts that much time and attention into something, you can't help learning a thing or two about that task. In my case, the task has been determining what the factors are that contribute to a person's happiness. My acquired knowledge in working with people of all ages, from all walks of life, is about how to live happy. Every one of those thousands of therapy sessions with the most courageous people on earth-those who attend therapy-has contributed to my formula for a happy life. *That* is what enables me to tell you the fundamentals of achieving a happy life.

An Important Question

I have an important question to ask you. Do not read another word until you have an answer for yourself. Here's the question. What is the **one** thing that you want in your life that will make you happy? Is it financial independence? Is it more basic than that, such as good health? Maybe your answer is to have satisfying love in your life. Would having more friends do it for you? Your answer could be to have more time. Or is it simply to have a motorcycle? Would a ski house in Vail do the trick for you? Think about it. Really think about it. What would *your* answer be? So many people say that, "I would be happy if only I had . . ."

Whatever your answer is, it doesn't matter. It is a trick question because whatever that one thing is that you believe will make you happier, or change your life, it isn't the answer. Even if your answer was to simply be happy. It is far more complex and pervasive an experience to be happy. Achievement of happiness, freedom, and self-fulfillment is a multifaceted, complex endeavor. It is doubtful that it is one thing that will improve your life. I don't know if you are a football fan or not, but building a championship football team is an excellent example of a concept that is multifaceted and complex. As a General Manager, your job is to acquire players at all positions to potentiate a winning team. Some say you can't win without a great quarterback. Others purport winning teams must have a great defense. Still others say the key to winning is having an outstanding offensive line. The truth is that you need all those things. If you have a Peyton Manning quarterback but a terrible offensive line to protect him against being sacked, your great quarterback can't play his best. If your defense is poor the opposing team scores a lot of points which puts the pressure on your offense to score a lot of points. Every position and aspect of the game, including special teams play, affects every other dimension of the game and how each player performs.

Not a football fan? Ok. Everyone has seen a movie. Good movies and bad movies. Have you ever seen the credits at the end of a film? They can go on for several minutes, listing all of the people in front of the camera and behind the scenes that make that movie a great movie. It can never be just having a great actor playing the lead role or the most talented director that makes a movie great. It requires a great script, great casting, directing, cinematography, editing, set location, etc.

Your life must be conducted in a similar way. You cannot focus on one or even two things to make your life happier. But the good news is that you only have to focus on only three things at any given time. You will undoubtedly understand what I mean once you have completed this book.

What Will It Take To Make You Happy?

What does it take to be happy? Happiness is one of our ultimate goals in life. Yet, I see people all around, in my personal life and patients in my office, who are just not happy. We often get caught up in our fast paced, complex lives, keeping happiness a distant, elusive goal instead of something we experience. People seem to be looking for something that is either missing or they just don't know what it is that will make them happy. Many people actually know what will make them happy yet they have no idea how to go about making it happen. Using my knowledge of the most inner workings of people's minds and being privy to their intimate lives for over four decades I have formulated a life guide that will help you live your life with quality, better relationships, less conflict, and less stress. At the core of this model for a life script is a mathematical thread involving, of all things, the number "3."

The Magic "3"

Several years ago I noticed a pattern in the interventions I used with my patients. Very often I would see that to make a significant change in whatever aspect of their life we were focusing on, there were three things they needed to change with respect to that issue. A 42-year-old patient named Arthur is just one example of many.

Arthur was having some difficulty with meeting deadlines in his rather demanding job. We identified all of the factors that were impeding his ability to get his work done on time. There were many, including over socializing in the office, staying up late, procrastination, not delegating certain tasks out to his direct reports, and misjudging the amount of time required to complete reports. If we altered only one of these impediments he would undoubtedly continue to experience difficulties. Making modifications for just two of these factors would also not be enough. Working on all of them would be too overwhelming, although eventually he would need to do so. We chose three. He began going to sleep earlier, which in turn, helped him with focus and concentration during his work day. He became more diligent with his electronic calendar assigning a date and time for each step required to complete a long range, multi-step task. Finally, his third change in the trio of modifications was to delegate more tasks to provide him with more time to focus on his time sensitive obligations.

It was always three things to make it a complete and comprehensive action plan. One suggestion was usually not enough. Two suggestions left room for error. Four was overwhelming or overkill. But three seemed to stand together, like a tripod. So, I started thinking about the number three in both a mathematical and practical sense.

In basic physics, a solid is comprised of 3 dimensions. For something to be solid, it requires length, width, and height. If one of these dimensions is missing, it no longer functions as a solid. Merely having length only gives you a line. Only having length and width provides a geometric plane, but add height and you have a solid. "Three" represents something that is *solid, real, substantial, complete,* and *entire*. For you to be *solid*, there are a series of "threes" that you need to attend to in various aspects of your life.

Your life consists of time. Time has 3 dimensions, past, present, and future-all of which need to be considered when attending to your happiness. Thoughts, words, and actions, is the "three" combination that we use to pursue happiness. Even our ecological domain is comprised of 3 elements – mineral, vegetable, and animal. There are 4 numbers that represent perfection with the number 3 being the first.

> *Three* represents divine perfection
> *Seven* represents spiritual perfection
> *Ten* represents ordinal perfection
> *Twelve* represents governmental perfection

Life Doesn't Have To Be Terrible

Malia, a 37-year-old woman, began therapy with me because she had the aching feeling that something was missing in her life. As I got to know and understand her, the initial feeling she presented was guilt. Malia was married, had two children and lived in an affluent town. She described her marriage as relatively happy. She and her husband had some marital problems 3 or 4 years prior to her seeing me but her husband made major changes. Still, she wasn't happy. Malia had the typical complaints about her two children including some sibling rivalry, homework battles from time to time, and having to ask them to clean their rooms 5 times until she had to yell and threaten punishment. That probably sounds sort of familiar to you. Malia was a full time homemaker and her family was financially secure. She had a limited social life because she felt very out of place in the upper middle class community in which she lived. Her own background included a similar socio-economic status, but she grew up in Texas. She found it difficult to relate to the values and culture of the New York metropolitan suburban stay-at-home mom. College educated with a degree in marketing and public relations, Malia initially identified feeling intellectually unfulfilled as being the piece that was missing in her life. As we explored her thoughts and feelings about this issue, it became apparent that renewing her career path that was purposefully shut down when she started having children was not the only issue. In fact, it wasn't even the real issue. Everything was good in Malia's life yet she felt a semblance of unhappiness. Everything was good but it just wasn't good enough. Comparing herself to less fortunate or overtly dysfunctional people in her life made her feel guilty for complaining. For years, she accepted her unhappiness because of that very fact. But, life doesn't have to be that terrible. And it doesn't have to be that average. Your life doesn't have to be mediocre, or boring, or less than what you fantasize it to be. Regardless of your specific situation there are things you can do to rectify the problem areas in your life, and improve the overall quality of your life.

When Things Are Just Not Going Well

Perhaps you feel like no matter what you do, trains keep leaving without you. You either can't seem to get out of your own way, or there seem to be obstacle after obstacle placed in front of you preventing you from being happy in your life. If you think you are a victim, never catching a break, it is time to stop the pity party and start to take control of your life. Maybe you are a victim. Or, could it be that you just make bad decisions and you create scenarios where the outcome tends to be a negative consequence for you? There is also a possibility that you view yourself as a victim as a defense mechanism. Seeing yourself as a victim and never catching a break can be a means of protection against really bad feelings. If you are the victim, you don't have to change. Change means you must confront your feelings and your actions to see the connection to the negative outcomes you tend to experience in your life. That may be a bit too difficult and emotionally threatening to your self-esteem. So, you become the victim both by not seeing your responsibility in creating bad situations and by feeling too emotionally tenuous to face the fact that you need to make changes. Reba is a perfect example.

Woe Is Me! It's A Pity Party

Reba, a 34-year-old woman works for a small civil engineering firm. She is smart, has a solid education from an esteemed college engineering program, and has better than average ability to help complete assigned projects. Reba complained that she was being passed up for promotions, did not get the maximum raise at her recent employee review, and only received half of her maximum bonus. Reba felt upset and angry. When asked why she thought this was happening she responded, "Well, it's hard to get ahead when you are the only woman in the group and the boss's son works there. So, Reba believes she is a victim of gender discrimination and nepotism. I asked Reba if it was possible that there was another explanation for her frustrating situation at work. I asked her about her colleagues and how they approached their work. She discovered that what she was not considering was that she was usually the last one in the office in the morning and was often the first to leave at the end of the day. Furthermore, she rarely did extra research for projects, rarely accepted invitations for dinners with perspective clients, and never attended political events that would enhance relationships with influential community leaders that authorize local projects. Her colleagues were doing all of these extra activities.

In reality, Reba was not going the extra mile which was the real reason for her lack of advancement and mediocre salary increases. She was quick to blame others instead of taking charge of her own growth at work. Continuing to believe that her gender and nepotism were the reasons for her work issues would only increase frustration and unhappiness. She felt helpless and discouraged but would not take any action to change it because she believed it was out of her locus of control.

Once Reba recognized her role and responsibility in her problem, she began to make the necessary changes. She changed the way she approached her job and gradually her efforts paid off both in salary and status among her colleagues.

Taking Charge Of Your Own Life

For you to achieve the triad of happiness, freedom, and self-fulfillment in your life, you must take charge of your own life. When I was doing my clinical training I had a wonderful mentor. He told me that he could see that I was very passionate about helping people and that I was going to be very successful as a psychologist. He felt the need to caution me saying, "Make sure you run your practice and do not let the practice run you." Are you running your life or is your life running you?

A core concept for your happiness is making sure you are taking charge of your life. So that the train doesn't leave without you, you need to be taking action, changing behavior patterns, and being proactive to head off problems. A common theme with patients is that they often feel trapped in their lives. That there is no way out with no options. Rarely, if ever, are there no options. Trapped is only a state of mind and is usually not a reality. Yes, sometimes the options aren't great options but, nevertheless, they can "untrap" you.

The Formula For Success
There are numerous subtle and significant changes you can make in your life to overcome problems, cope with stress, improve your present life, or simply promote self-growth. This book is the accumulation of the thousands of therapy sessions I have had with thousands of patients. I have found that there are certain common themes that apply to everyone's lives that can improve and enrich this one chance you have at making it all worthwhile. Anyone can benefit from my experience and everyone can better themselves using the formula I propose in the subsequent chapters.

I have identified the essential dimensions of daily living that are required to obtain happiness, freedom, and self-fulfillment. Remember, you need the trio-the 3 dimensions for matter to be solid – length, width, and height. If you are missing one of these dimensions it cannot be solid. With the number "3" applied to each of these critical areas of an individual's life there will always be 3 factors to address in order to acquire success in each area of your life. The total picture will help you navigate through life with less effort, less stress, and more happiness. Remember . . . you deserve to be happy. Mahatma Gandhi said that, "Happiness is when what you think, what you say, and what you do are in harmony." May I be so bold as to add one more piece to Gandhi's definition of happiness? It is also what you feel. Like Malia, even if your thinking, doing, and saying are in harmony, if you don't feel it, then something is missing or wrong. Collectively, each chapter in this book helps you make sure to fill in the gaps and solve the problems in your life.

CHAPTER 2
About Freedom

Freedom

Freedom is having independence and the options to do what you want to do, think how you want to think, live how you want to live, and feel the way you want to feel. Having freedom is so essential for happiness that I have devoted two chapters to it. Freedom is the ultimate luxury and like all luxuries, it must be earned. You are not entitled to live a free life, even if you live in a free society like America. You may be granted the opportunity of freedoms in a social and legal sense, but people create their own barriers in their relationships, their careers, and in their lives in general. It is these barriers that create unnecessary limits and box you in to the point that you feel trapped. When you live your life with as much freedom as you can muster, you are living a life that minimizes crisis, stress, and unhappiness. Of course, you can't completely eliminate bad things that happen. There is only so much you can control in your life. The realistic goal is to reduce the negativity and potentiate the success.

I refer to freedom in every sense of the word and every aspect of the definition. From how you spend your time and with whom you spend it. What you buy and where you go. Whether you take a vacation or a stay-cation. Choosing the kind of work you do and with whom you work with is freedom. Freedom is happiness. Freedom is freeing. Free from limits, boundaries and psychological chains that make us feel like we are trapped or that the train keeps leaving without us in our life.

The word "free" strikes excitement in most people. If you pass a deli counter and you see a sign that says, "Free Samples" something stirs inside of you. You can get something for doing nothing. "Free" means that it doesn't cost you anything. "Free" means you don't have obligations or responsibility to obtain whatever it is that is free. "Free Weights" do not mean that the exercise tool doesn't cost any money. It means that you can use the weights without the limitations of cables or bars attached to them. It means that there aren't limits that hold you back. The amount of freedom you create in your life has a direct impact on the amount of happiness you will have in your life. Obtaining freedom in your life involves some very specific components. The following is a list of the "freedom components."

- Power
- Options
- Opportunity
- Ability
- Flexibility
- Exemption
- Growth

Interestingly, these components have a circuitous relationship with freedom in your life. They are not only the way to achieve freedom, but having freedom also allows you to have these components. So implementing them gives you freedom, and freedom in your life enables you to possess them.

Power

What comes to mind when you think of having power? Do you readily associate the idea of having great strength with power? If you have power does that enable you to get what you want? Does the notion of having power afford you high status? Or, is power more of a skill that helps you control other people in your life? These are all external types of power and aspects or consequences of having power. But, there is a much more powerful power than having great strength, getting what you want, having status, and getting people to do what you want them to do. It is having the power over yourself. This type of power is internal power.

Having internal power and control over yourself is the type of power that helps you obtain true freedom. Internal power gives you a feeling of self-empowerment and is completely contingent upon your own thoughts, feelings, and actions. External power is heavily reliant on the reactions of others and their perception of you. External power is dependent upon what others do so without their desired reaction you will not have power. External power is either taken by force or it is given to you after you earn it. The problem with external power is that since it is contingent upon others reaction to you in some way, the power can be usurped or taken away by them.

Internal power is not taken by force and cannot be given to you. Internal power is developed, nurtured, and is independent of others. Internal power is the greatest power you can possess in your life because it makes you impervious to external stressors and unpleasant circumstances. Internal power is completely dependent on *you* and at the end of the day, cannot be usurped or taken away by others.

Developing Internal Power

Your ability to cope with everything in your life begins with what you think and what you believe about yourself and the world around you. Your thoughts and beliefs determine how you feel and subsequently how you are going to act or behave.

Randy, a 16-year-old patient had a crush on Melissa. He had never asked a girl out before and he expressed his tremendous anxiety about doing so. Randy verbalized self- deprecating remarks to me such as, "Why would she go out with me? I am not in the popular group, her last boyfriend was on the football team, and she probably thinks I am just a fencing geek." Although somewhat common for an adolescent boy experiencing a combination of hormone rush and insecurities, you can clearly see how his thoughts were affecting how he felt about himself, the situation, and what he was actually doing with his crush on Melissa-which was nothing. His lack of confidence driven by self-doubting thoughts immobilized him to the point where he had difficulty even talking to her even though she sat next to him in his Algebra II class. His negative thoughts caused him anxiety and subsequent inaction making him feel trapped within his own mind. This is not freedom. Randy needed the power, the internal power, to change this situation to give him a chance at happiness.

The first step was to challenge and change Randy's negative thoughts and beliefs about how attractive he might be to Melissa, and girls in general. We examined the evidence of reality instead of the irrational inner world he created about how girls see him. True, he had never asked a girl out before but he did have several girls as close friends. They seem to like being around him, texted, talked, and invited him to social gatherings. They laugh at his jokes and seem to enjoy confiding in him regarding their own problems. Next, Randy had to repeatedly remind himself of his great attributes such as his kind, caring personality, his intelligence, and his keen sense of humor. Randy began to think about himself as the kind of person that girls like to be around, and that he had personality traits that girls seem to enjoy. Changing his inner thoughts was the first step toward giving himself power.

The second step was to begin to implement a plan. This involved some role playing and behavioral rehearsal so that his fear of fumbling and stuttering when he finally spoke to her would not occur. Randy had to begin to have a conversation with Melissa if he was eventually going to ask her out.

Randy gradually mustered up the courage to begin speaking to Melissa before and after their math class. As it turns out, he did find out from a mutual friend that Melissa was talking a lot about "this boy that sits next to [her] in math class." He got her cell number, became Instagram friends, and he eventually asked her to get together.

Instead of giving in to his self-defeating attitude Randy decided to take the power and approach his problem instead of just complain and feel badly about it. His internal power gave him the ability to create happiness, freedom, and self-fulfillment to get something that he really wanted-to date Melissa.

Randy's train did not leave without him because he took internal control over himself and that resulted in a successful outcome.

Options

Having options in your life gives you freedom and having freedom gives you the ability to choose people, places, and things in your life. It gives you options so that you don't feel trapped and depressed. It is a common sense mathematical concept. Having options creates a better chance that you will end up with a positive outcome. If you went to a restaurant and there were only 4 entrées on the menu, the chance that you will be eating something that you really like is much less likely compared to a restaurant with a menu with twenty options.

You need to create options in your life to prevent feeling boxed in. Providing yourself with options in your life means making choices among different alternatives. More often than not those choices are very difficult to make. It may mean choosing to give up positive options for even better ones. Or, you may need to choose the least negative option out of all negative choices. It also means choosing to eliminate people in your life that do not contribute positively to the quality of your life or your happiness.

How you spend your time and with whom you spend it with is part of the greatest freedom you can achieve. The old adage, "You can choose your friends but you can't choose your family," does hold true. However, living a life with a sense of freedom gives you the option of ending negative social relationships and setting limits in negative family relationships. I am not an advocate of terminating a family relationship unless it is toxic to your mental health. However, you can limit the amount of time you spend and talk to that family member. And, you can refuse to allow them to make you feel badly or guilty.

Choosing the type of job you do and with whom you work with is freedom. Bill, a Ph.D. chemist was working for a large pharmaceutical company. He entered therapy due to depression and quality of life issues. Bill has a wife and 2 children, 12 and 14- years-old. He consistently complained about his job, working in a lab to develop new medications. When Bill initially starting working for this company 14 years ago, it was a prominent sought after drug company for biochemists to work for. The laboratory resources seemed limitless, the salary and benefits were generous, and the professional development perks were liberal. In recent years, the increase in FDA regulations, sinking economy, and intense competition in the industry caused his company to make significant changes in the way they do business and what they were offering their employees. Those changes created an undesirable and frustrating work environment for Bill. On top of that, his immediate supervisor, mandated with maintaining strict project budgets, was demanding and negative. Bill no longer felt happy going to work. We decided that this was the major source of his unhappiness and depression. It was no longer fun and interesting going to work due to the lack of resources, limited pay increases, low morale in the environment, and the lack of support from his boss.

Over time, it became clear to Bill that he needed to make a change. He decided to explore the possibility of teaching high school chemistry. He discovered that he could become certified through the alternative teaching certificate route rather easily. He also discovered that the job market for high school chemistry teachers was excellent. Unfortunately, there would be some trade-offs. A significant salary cut was the primary issue, with a substantial mortgage and college creeping up in the near future for his oldest son. Nevertheless, Bill saw the positives as clearly outweighing the negatives. The impact of his work would once again be meaningful. His vacations would coincide with his children's school schedules. With summers off, he could do consulting work to supplement his income. He would have the independence to run his classroom in a way that made sense, instead of trying to run his lab with the numerous cost cutting constraints his pharmaceutical corporation put into place over the past few years. Bill made the change and it actually turned out better than he expected.

Bill complained and believed he had no options, that he was trapped. His unhappiness was sort of a double unhappiness. He was upset about his job and he was depressed about feeling trapped in it. Once he realized he did have options, he became encouraged and empowered. Once he changed jobs, he became free of the negativity, felt self-fulfilled, and happy.

Opportunity

As you may be beginning to see, the elements of freedom are not mutually exclusive. One creates the other which enables another. Using your internal power leads to options and taking options feeds your ability to have internal power. When you are using your internal power and creating options for yourself, you also create opportunities. Being in the right place at the right time gives you the ability to take advantage of opportunities. Having different opportunities offers you a better chance at freedom, self-fulfillment, and happiness.

Some people look at others and say, "He is so lucky. He has a great job, a happy marriage, health, and not a care in the world." If you say that about other people, then your train might keep leaving without you. There is such a thing as luck and it can be good luck or bad luck. But the kind of luck you have is largely due to your own actions. If you are taking control over your own actions, you can put yourself in a position to be able to capitalize on opportunities.

A colleague once said to me, "You are so lucky to get invited to so many speaking engagements across the country. You get to share so much information to so many people, and get paid well to do it!" I thought about his view of "luck" and became annoyed with it. What I did was, wrote a book, *Generation Text*, which happened to be an extremely hot and cutting edge topic at the time. It took 2 years of meetings, research, writing, and editing *Generation Text* before the first book actually hit the shelf. From there I was sought out by the media, including interviews and appearances on numerous TV, radio, and print magazines. It was a great 7-year ride and I was "lucky" to have experienced it. But, it wasn't luck. I took an idea and instead of just thinking about it I took action. I put the idea on paper, pitched it to a colleague who was well published, who connected me to her literary agent. I created an opportunity by taking action.

Freedom offers opportunities and opportunities give you more freedom. Once again, it is circuitous. It puts you in places and situations that can really pay off for you. Can you think of an example when you gave yourself "good luck" or an opportunity to benefit yourself? Maybe you volunteered to do something above and beyond your scope at work. That gave you visibility to someone who became impressed with you. Perhaps that person was in a position of authority and recruited you for a better, more interesting job within the company. How "lucky" would that be?

Ability

Freedom gives you the ability to demonstrate your skills and knowledge to yourself and others. Utilizing your skills often gives you freedom. It gives you the power to have options and opportunities.

Randy, was a 27-year-old patient who was very self-conscious, anxious, and had low self-esteem. She had enjoyed doing some backstage work on high school theatre productions but could not muster up the courage to audition for on-stage parts. She became intrigued when she saw an advertisement for an open audition for a community theatre musical production. Randy always had a great singing voice according to family but never sang in public. She decided to use this community theatre opportunity to overcome her anxiety and lack of self-confidence. We worked on challenging her irrational beliefs about her voice not being good enough, and the possibility of being ridiculed and embarrassed. Randy auditioned and although she didn't get the part she was seeking, she was accepted for an ensemble group appearing in three scenes. Receiving a part on stage validated the quality of her singing voice. "They would not have chosen me if my voice wasn't at least decent," she reasoned.

The ability to sing gave Randy the freedom to audition for other plays. Her talent freed her up to pursue a hobby that she not only enjoyed, but helped her improve self-esteem and overcome anxiety. Randy's ability to sing turned out to be a vehicle to expand her world and give her a freedom that she had never had.

Flexibility

If you have the freedom to be flexible it means that you are receptive to modification and change. Flexibility enables you to bend without breaking.

You are adaptable and pliable yet there is still a modicum of substance and solidity. The opposite of flexibility is rigidity. Ironically, if you are a flexible person you have the ability to choose to be rigid when you need to be firm or unyielding. If you are a rigid person, it is difficult for you to be flexible. Flexibility gives you the freedom to be rigid when you need to be steadfast. Freedom allows you to be flexible when you want to be flexible. Flexibility and rigidity both have their appropriate place in specific situations without unnecessary limitations. Think about a rubber band and a pencil-two common objects found in most homes. The rubber band is flexible and can fit into many spaces of different shapes and sizes. It can be applied to various tasks such as grouping papers, holding two objects together, and functioning mechanically in a gadget. It melds and bends to adapt to many applications. A pencil, however, is rigid. It can function as a writing instrument but has limited use in other situations. The rigidity of a pencil does have its place. After all, you can't write with a rubber band. But if you have the freedom to use the rubber band or pencil when you want to, then it gives you the ability to accomplish your task successfully.

Think about parenting with regard to flexibility. As a parent you have the freedom to make rules for your children. Good parenting sometimes means standing firm (rigid) with those rules so that the child learns to comply with them. Great parenting knows when it is appropriate to be flexible and break the rule. For example, if the rule is that iPads are forbidden in the bedroom after 8:00 PM on a school night, that rule must be consistently enforced. Kids sneakily play games on their iPad when it should be lights out and bedtime. But what if your child is running a fever, is uncomfortable and is just feeling crumby? As a parent, you have the freedom to be flexible and adapt to the situation by allowing her to have her iPad to help her feel more comfortable and take her mind off of her physical discomfort.

Flexibility provides you with the ability to reduce the amount of limitations and trapped feelings in your life. It enables you power, options, provides more opportunities, enhances your abilities, and promotes self-growth leading to more freedom, happiness, and self-fulfillment.

Exemption

Did you ever take a high school or college course and the instructor's policy was that if you have an "A" going into the final exam that you can be exempt from taking that final exam? In reality, by taking care of your responsibilities in that class you earn the right to be exempt. You earned immunity from a requirement that others need to meet. Exemption gives you the freedom to opt out of many requirements and activities that you find unpleasant, uninteresting, or drudgery. Exemption is usually earned or obtained in some way, and can give you privileges that others do not have.

A perfect example is the TSA Pre Check program that the Transportation Security Administration offers to airplane passengers. If you take the time to complete the application, attend an in-person screening, and pay a fee, you become exempt from specific security requirements at United States airports. Having the TSA Pre Check means that when you go through security prior to getting to your gate you are afforded exemptions that everyone else has to comply with. Your line is significantly shorter, you are not required to remove your shoes and belt, computers can remain in their cases, jackets can be worn, and the 3 oz. liquid limitation is not applied. Exemption gives you convenience and privilege.

Try not to think of exemption as a "snobby" concept reserved only for the rich and famous. Exemption is freedom and takes many forms during the course of your life on many levels. Examples of exemptions may be:

- A 15% discount on the clothes you purchase at the retail store where you work
- The ability to pre-purchase hard to get concert tickets because you are in good standing with your American Express credit card
- The owner of a local restaurant you frequent gives you a complimentary after dinner drink that everyone else has to pay for.
- Your men's softball team is given a "buy" for the first round of the play-offs because you had the best record in the league.

Exemption comes in many shapes and sizes but almost always gives you the freedom to choose, make your life easier, more convenient, or comfortable in some way.

Growth

When you have all of the components that freedom yields, you will have growth. Growth is the culmination or natural by-product of freedom. Growth is the natural result when all of the positive forces of freedom are working together. When you are empowering yourself, choosing options, seizing opportunities, accessing and utilizing your abilities, exercising flexibility, and taking advantage of exemptions, you are destined to keep growing. Fortunately, your growth will more often than not be growth in a positive direction. Even if your growth opens up new avenues for you that do not work out positively, it still keeps you on a path toward freedom, happiness, and self-fulfillment because you can then eliminate that negative avenue from your life.

Growth means that you are ever developing without being stagnant. Growth prevents feeling stifled and the feeling that you are trapped in your unhappy situation. Growth prevents boredom and depression. As you experience continual growth achievement, self-improvement, and success become an increasing phenomena in your life.

Barbara, a 56-year-old married woman felt very dependent on her husband. By her report, her husband was not controlling and very much wanted her to become more independent. Barbara grew up in a traditional family that did not encourage independence in girls. As a result, Barbara would rely on her husband to take care of things such as arranging home repairs, driving longer distances for social engagements, and the household finances. Five years ago, her husband received a promotion requiring him to travel for 3-4 days at a time. The need to attend to financial matters and household maintenance issues increased in frequency while he was away on his business trips. Barbara began to feel anxious while he was away, worrying about not being capable of taking care of issues as they arose. She also started to feel somewhat lonely, socially, because she could no longer rely on her husband to drive her to their friends' houses that lived some distance away.

Barbara decided that she had to become more self-sufficient. She purchased a GPS for her car to allay her fear of getting lost when driving to long distance friends' homes. She, with her husband's help, compiled a list of repairmen and their phone numbers according to skill. She had her husband explain how he had been managing the monthly bills, their savings, and investments and took it over. Her independence stimulated her growth. Barbara felt a new found feeling of competence and began taking control over her own life. This generalized to other areas of her life which in turn increased her self-esteem. With increased independence she experienced increased growth. This freed her up to take advantage of many more social and personal opportunities that she had previously turned down.

The Importance of Freedom

Freedom, and all that goes with it, is so essential for your happiness. However, it is important to note that ultimate freedom is virtually impossible. To some degree, there will always be boundaries and parameters limiting your options. Sometimes it is a legal limitation, or a practical boundary, or a physical barrier, or it is the cost of hurting someone else that puts the lid on your freedom. The idea is to obtain as much as you can, and experience freedom within those other imposed limitations. Obtaining freedom can be complicated and difficult, depending on your individual circumstances. However, it is so important that I have devoted the next two chapters to try to simplify what you need to do to approach having freedom in your life.

CHAPTER 3

Achieving Freedom-
Part I

Health Money*Knowledge*

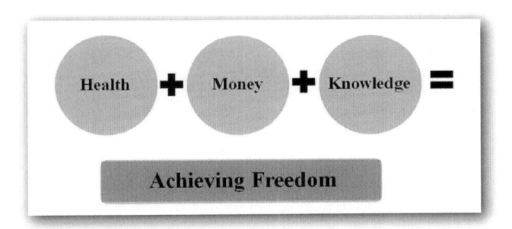

Health

L eigh Hunt, an English poet, said, "The groundwork of all happiness is
health." Anything you try to accomplish in your life starts and ends
with your health. If you have ever been ill, even for just a day or so,
you know you cannot function the way you normally do. Having a chronic

medical condition, especially when it involves pain, inhibits your productivity and negatively affects your mood. Besides illnesses and medical conditions, if you are merely not in good physical shape, you more than likely are not performing up to par.

Being in good health increases your stamina, improves concentration, and gives you a competitive edge that keeps you sharp in your thinking and in physical execution of any task.

Being in good health gives you freedom to conduct your life without physical restrictions you would experience if you are in poor health.

Rob, a 45-year-old accountant, takes his family on vacation every year after working long hours every day for 4 months straight during tax season. He is a dedicated husband and father and tries to make up for his absence from his family. His most recent trip was to Costa Rica with several adventures and excursions planned with his wife and two teenage boys in mind. There were two long hikes involving hills and rocks to scale, walks along the beach, zip lining, horseback riding, and a bike trip. His wife and sons had a wonderful time exploring and enjoying all of these very physical activities, with the exception of his wife and the zip lining. Her fear took over even though she was glad she did it in the end. Rob, however, struggled with all of these activities due to his physical condition. It was more like his physical "un-condition" because Rob was 30 pounds overweight and very out of shape. His lung capacity and lack of muscle tone caused him to focus on getting through these activities instead of enjoying the experience of them. He couldn't smell the roses because he was beleaguered with heavy breathing and aches and pains in his arms and legs. Rob hid his physical frustration from his family but it prevented him from sharing the exhilarating fun that his family was obviously experiencing. It saddened him, both because he couldn't be in the moment with his family, and because he mentally beat himself up due to his lack of physical health. Rob's lack of physical health created limitations on his Costa Rica vacation. It was an imaginary box that he inadvertently placed himself in. If he had been maintaining his physical health he would have been free to enjoy it at the same level as his wife and sons did. There is that word again-"free." It was a wake-up call for Rob.

Physical Health

The first building block for freedom is to maintain your physical health. Being physically fit sets your body up to meet all of your daily challenges. So many patients say to me, "Dr. Osit, I know I need to work out but I just can't find the time to do it." My response is that time cannot be found. Time is an interesting concept and will be dealt with later in this chapter when we discuss money as a means to achieve freedom. But this patient, and you, just can't *find* time as if it was hiding or elusive. You must *make* the time in your weekly schedule to exercise and maintain your physical health.

To do so, a regular exercise routine needs to be incorporated into your weekly schedule. There are various philosophies for how much, how often, what type of exercise you should be doing at different ages. I don't think the specific program you choose matters as much as doing something instead of nothing. Workouts should be part of your routine during the week, no matter how busy you are. I have never met anyone, and remember, I have seen thousands of patients over the years, who couldn't steal 20-30 minutes from 3 or 4 days of their week from a nonproductive or time wasting activity to be able to exercise. Once it becomes a routine in your life it happens almost automatically. You brush your teeth, you shower, you eat your meals, you sleep, you put your keys in that kitchen drawer, and you work out. It is just part of what you need to do. Working out regularly gives you the advantage of putting yourself in a place that maximizes your productivity and minimizes your health risk.

Sleep

Another important aspect in maintaining your health is sleep. When your brain and body receive the proper amount of sleep it sets you up for both physical and emotional health. Sleeping well and sleeping enough can also help your body recover from medical illness and physical injuries. Inadequate sleep habits are associated with:

- depression
- poor concentration
- irritability
- lack of sustained attention span
- obesity
- diabetes
- heart disease

It is still somewhat of a scientific mystery as to why people need sleep, but studies using animals as subjects indicate that sleep is necessary for survival. Researchers studying various aspects of sleep deprivation in rats indicate some rather dramatic results. Rats live, on average, for 2 to 3 years. However, when they are deprived of their sleep they only live about 3 weeks. When they are deprived of Rapid Eye Movement (REM) sleep their life span is reduced to about 5 weeks. When deprived of sleep, rats also maintain abnormally low body temperatures and develop sores on their bodies. Additionally, it was found that their immune systems were compromised when deprived of sleep. With humans, the amount of sleep deprivation is sometimes referred to as "sleep debt." Analogous to a financial debt, at some point in time it needs to be repaid. When you continually lose sleep the body requires you to replace that lost sleep.

Sleep seems to be directly related to how our neurological system functions. Inadequate sleep patterns create a foggy cognitive state, affects memory, information retrieval, and concentration. This also translates into decreased physical performance. Your overall competence and abilities are consequently impaired, limiting your chance for internal power, options, and opportunities throughout your day.

How Much Sleep Do We Need?
The amount of sleep required varies from person to person, as well as the age of the person. The following chart is the generally agreed upon amount of sleep for various ages.

Age	Hours of Sleep
Birth to 1-year-old	14-16
1-3 years-old	12-14
3-6	10-12
7-12	10-11
12-18	8-9
Adults	7-8

Figure 1. Sleep Required By Age

The ABC's of ZZZs

In 2015 the National Sleep Foundation recommended maintaining healthy "sleep hygiene" to improve the quality of your life (http://sleepfoundation.org/sleep-tools-tips/healthy-sleep-tips, 2015). They listed 10 recommendations to consistently employ for good sleep hygiene.

1. Establish and stick to a consistent schedule for your bedtime and wake up time. This is recommended even on non-work or school days in order to maintain a healthy circadian rhythm, or sleep cycle.
2. Establish relaxing bedtime rituals every night prior to going to bed. These activities should be low key, relaxing, and conducted away from bright lights. Playing video games, surfing the Internet, and high activity games should be avoided. Reading is an activity that can be calming and conducive for preparing your body for rest.
3. Avoid naps during the day. Power naps are permissible only if you do not have trouble falling asleep at night.
4. Exercise daily with either vigorous or light exercise. The time of day does not matter as long as exercising does not interfere with your sleep.
5. Make sure your sleep environment is conducive for a good sleep. Your bedroom temperature should be between 60 and 67 degrees. It should be free from noise and light distractions. The use of blackout lights, eye shades, ear plugs, white noise machines, humidifiers, and

fans can facilitate a good sleep and help you if you are having difficulty sleeping.

6. Your mattress and pillows should be comfortable and supportive. Your bed should be a place that feels "good" when you get into it at night. Older mattresses might not support your body in a way that is conducive for sleep.

7. To maintain your circadian rhythm, or healthy sleep cycles, avoid being in bright light in the evening. Bright light stimulates the brain and "tricks" it into thinking it is awake time instead of sleep time. Try to receive bright sunlight during the day, as well.

8. Avoid eating large meals within 2-3 hours of bedtime. Large meals, spicy foods, and liquids that contain caffeine could make falling asleep difficult. Alcohol and cigarettes should also be avoided.

9. Everyone has difficulty falling asleep at some point. But if you have consistent trouble falling asleep, try to associate your bed with just two activities – sleep and sex. Maintain a sleep diary in an effort to ascertain common patterns or issues regarding your sleep habits. If you continue to have trouble sleeping, consult your physician or contact a sleep disorder specialist.

10. There are relatively inexpensive technological devices such as the Fit Bit that provides a tremendous amount of information about how you sleep. These devices can be very useful in making adjustments in your sleep patterns and sleep hygiene.

Diet and Eating Habits

In addition to maintaining your physical health and sleep habits, your diet and eating habits are another fundamental aspect of having good health. If you are overweight, dieting to lose weight is a very frustrating endeavor. If you have an alcohol problem, or a gambling problem, you can eliminate alcohol or gambling activities from your life and live very nicely. An alcoholic or addicted gambler still has tremendous difficulty eliminating these activities from their life, but temptation can be avoided in many ways. With dieting, you cannot eliminate food from your life. Hunger and the fact that you need to eat for sustenance make it doubly hard to limit your caloric intake and eat the proper foods for weight loss because you have constant temptation and the need to gratify your hunger. The smartest thing you can do is not let yourself gain the weight in the first place. In any event, maintaining a proper, well balanced diet will enhance your energy level and mental acuity. It is part of the total health picture, which is one of the triad of components to achieve freedom.

Losing weight or maintaining a healthy weight can be a very individual process. I am, by no means, a diet expert but in working with countless patients regarding their feelings about their weight and how they attempt to lose or maintain a healthy body, I have concluded that first and foremost, diet has to be a way of life, not a specific program. Secondly, diet programs, if they are used, must be easily incorporated into your present lifestyle with only minor adjustments or else you probably will never maintain it.

Mental Health

Mental health is the core element of this book. Obviously, one section in one chapter in a book isn't going to provide you with what you need to maintain good mental health. If you incorporate all of the information on these pages, it will provide you with the framework for mental health. I believe that you should go for a mental health "checkup" once a year with a qualified clinician just as you would for your yearly physical with your Internist. We all "hide" feelings and issues from ourselves and become so engrossed in the craziness of our lives that we lose perspective. I will address having perspective more in depth in Chapter 6. Having a yearly mental health checkup will help you stay on track, make adjustments before they grow into problems or dysfunction, and head off potentially developing situations or relationships that could become problematic.

Suffice to say at this juncture, that mental health is the last component of maintaining your health which leads to freedom. Achieving mental health is an extremely complex and multifaceted process. It is also a life-long process.

So for now, just keep in mind that it basically requires carving time out for you, as well as balancing your work schedule, time spent with friends, your partner, and family.

If You Are Dealt A Bad Hand With Health

Never take health for granted. It is not valued until illness comes, and then it is too late. The health dimension in the triad of Health/Money/Knowledge is wonderful if you do not have a chronic medical condition, physical disability, sleep disorder, or mental illness. But, not everyone is blessed with a disability free body. Most disabilities will either make it impossible, or at least difficult to attend to all of the aspects of your health the way I am suggesting you do.

Carl, a 16-year-old high school student suffers from a rare autoimmune disease. It is a systemic culprit that affects his sleep, appetite, energy level, and concentration. It is the kind of illness that allows him to have a string of symptom free days followed by an inability to get out of bed due to fatigue, headache, and physical weakness. Needless to say, Carl misses a great deal of school due to his chronic illness. Carl needs to battle this malady every day of his life, making it difficult to lead a healthy lifestyle. He does not eat well, sleep well, get physical exercise, and has little to no social life with friends due to lack of energy. Carl had a conscious decision to make. He had to decide between being miserable and complain about not having a normal teenager's life, or make the best of his situation and enjoy what he could of his teenage life. He chose the latter. Whenever Carl had a string of good days he made sure he would connect with his friends. When he wasn't feeling well, he used social media and online video gaming to stay connected and have fun with his friends. He never discussed his medical issues with his friends because he did not want them to treat him any differently than the other guys in his friend group.

Carl would exercise on good days, which was part of his treatment regimen. He maintained a gluten free diet even though he disliked the taste of gluten free products. In other words, instead of "woe is me," Carl adopted an attitude that included making the best of his situation and making his medical situation the best it could be.

You have the same two choices that Carl has if you are dealt a lousy medical hand. You can either make the best of it or be miserable. It is a conscious choice. Having the medical issue is something you do not have control over. You do have control over your attitude and actions. Taking this type of control in your life will avoid having the train leave without you.

Money

If you subscribe to the notion that money is the root of all evil, then it will be very difficult for you to live in America or any other society where money is the primary barter exchange. As you read this section, try to throw any predisposed, subjective negative judgments about money and its relationship to powerful people, arrogant people, snobby people, and privileged people. Think of money as a good thing. It is one of the 3 components necessary to gain freedom in your life.

I know what you are thinking. "Is he saying that you need money to be happy?" Well, of course I'm not saying that. But if you have a choice between being poor and being wealthy, which would you choose? You don't need money to be happy. When my wife and I were first married and I was in one of my 9 years of graduate training, we didn't live on much. We had to decline many invitations with friends to go out to dinner or even to the movies, due to our limited funds. Instead, we spent many Saturday nights spending $7.00 on a cheap bottle of wine and a bag of potato chips playing backgammon. We had fun and we enjoyed the moment. Today, we have a few more dollars in our pocket and we go to a very special restaurant on our anniversary every year and spend between $800 and $1000 on dinner. We have fun and we enjoy the moment. It's not the amount of money you spend, it is how you spend your time. When we were living on our extremely limited budget we used the money to augment our time together. Now, we still use the few extra dollars in our pocket to spend time together.

You may be confused right now because it sounds as if I am talking out of both sides of my mouth. Two paragraphs ago it sounded as if I was saying you need money to be happy and find freedom in your life. Now, it seems like I am saying you don't need money to be happy and find freedom in your life. What I am really trying to convey is that you don't need money to be happy and find freedom, but having money provides you with more choices and options to enhance your life experiences. My wife and I enjoy each other's company no matter how much our Saturday night costs. But, having the ability to choose which restaurant we go to and only needing to look at the left side of the menu page (not the prices on the right) eliminates any restricted feelings while enjoying our time together. You can enjoy a ride in the country in a Toyota Corolla, but isn't it even more enjoyable in a Bugatti with the top down?

How Money Can Limit Your Freedom

Money gives you choices and enables you to enjoy what you want to enjoy instead of what you *have* to enjoy. When money is used to impress people it will often create limits and restrictions in your life. For example, if you purchase a house that is beyond your comfortable financial means, you can become house poor. It may be a big, beautiful home that others may be in awe of when they visit. What your visitors don't know is that the insane amount of money you borrowed from the bank creating a huge financial nut every month causes you to give up many other necessities and luxuries. The impressive house prevents you from taking a yearly vacation, causes you to be late on other monthly expenses, creates stress and tension between you and your spouse, and makes you scrutinize almost all of the purchases you make during the month, remembering that you need to have the money to meet that colossal mortgage payment.

Another example is if you gamble your money either in the stock market or in the casino. Most gamblers lose. When you lose the money you already have you are virtually stealing freedom from yourself by not only limiting other choices in your life, but you may be limiting relationships, as well. The idea is to use the money you have so that it increases your freedom, not decreases it. The first thing you need to do is to consciously decide what your philosophy is about earning, spending and saving your money. There needs to be a healthy balance among earning, spending, and saving money.

A Healthy Balance

There is no magic or revelation concept I can present regarding managing your money. It is simple and it is practical. Nor is there anything magical about how to create a healthy balance between earning, spending, and saving money. Nevertheless, the obvious must be stated so that it might at the very least stimulate your thinking about how you are handling the money part of obtaining freedom.

You can't spend the majority of your time earning money. For most people, the more time spent on their job the more money they will earn. If you are paid hourly that is self-evident. Even if you are paid an established yearly salary, working more hours usually translates into more money when bonus, raise, and promotion time comes around. Following the idea that money creates freedom, one would think that I would recommend working as much as you can to earn as much money as you can. The problem is that for every hour you work it takes an hour away from the other parts and people in your life.

You can spend all of your money, yielding lots of choices in your life. Having choices is something I am clearly advocating for. Of course, spending very little money limits your choices. Again, you need to strike a balance between how much money you spend in relation to how much money you make.

You can also save all of your money once your bills are paid, or you can spend all of it. Saving all of it will limit your freedom and create a restrictive lifestyle. Saving none of your money will give you lots of freedom in your present life, but cause massive limitations later in life or if you experience a financial setback with loss of income. You need to strike a balance between your earnings and savings.

One way to easily determine how much balance you are achieving with your money is to create and maintain a line item budget, keeping track of your earnings, expenditures, and savings. This is easily accomplished using an Excel spreadsheet or similar software. If you are not adept at spreadsheet software applications, then a good old fashioned graph paper and pencil will certainly do.

First, record the number of hours you are working each month. Don't fool yourself. Be honest about your hours. Record the amount of sleep you are getting, as well. What is left is your discretionary or "play" time. What do those proportions look like? Are you getting enough leisure time? Do you have too much time and can increase your work time or get another part-time job to increase your income?

Next, keep track of your after tax monthly earnings. And lastly, categorize every dollar that leaves your wallet. Make sure you list all of the categories and be very meticulous about accounting for every dollar you are spending. Maintain this spreadsheet and analyze it periodically to determine errant patterns or adjustments that need to be made. Remember, the idea is to create balance between earning, spending, and saving your money to optimize your freedom.

Money And Time

There is one last piece of wisdom about the relationship between money and freedom. Money and time are similar concepts. You can spend both money and time. Both have finite limits in availability. You can budget both to make the most out of them. You can waste both. You can donate both money and time. But there is one difference that is very important for you to understand and live by. You can take a dollar out of your pocket and spend it, and in return, earn that dollar back and place it right back in your pocket. The important understanding about time is that once you spend a minute doing something, you cannot replace that minute like you can replace the dollar. You can earn more money but you cannot earn more time. That makes it more valuable than money, and should be treated as a precious commodity as you go through your life.

I was sitting in a session once with a 13-year-old patient and his father. His father delivered a lecture on some inane, minor problem he was having with his son. When he was finished the boy turned to his father and said in a very calm voice, "You just wasted a minute of my life." I thought about that response. He was correct. And that minute cannot be replaced. So don't waste minutes.

Knowledge

The third dimension in creating as much freedom in your life as possible is knowledge. One of the most powerful tools to possess in your life is to have knowledge. Having knowledge is tantamount to having power. Not the kind of power that dominates others, or power in the sense of strength. It is the kind of power that gives you freedom to think for yourself. With knowledge, you can make intelligent decisions because you can weigh the options and think critically. Having information is one aspect of having knowledge. The real power comes in your ability to think critically and analyze. The ability to acquire information, think critically, and intelligently analyze can be applied to all aspects of your life.

Acquiring Knowledge

One of the most important quests in your life needs to be acquiring as much knowledge as you can. No matter what your age, gaining knowledge helps you have as much freedom as possible. There are several ways to acquire knowledge throughout your life. An obvious and primary means of acquiring knowledge is through formal education. Formal education can be sought through any program conferring academic degrees at any level, and various programs such as certifications, licensure, and skilled crafts such as electrician, plumber, woodworker, welder, etc.

Formal education is not the only means of acquiring knowledge. By making sure you are an observer of life experiences and people you encounter you can enhance your informational and social knowledge.

Observation is a powerful means of acquiring knowledge throughout your life. Active listening is yet another form of education that helps you acquire knowledge. Using a watch, listen, and learn mindset will help you increase your knowledge about yourself and how the world works to help you navigate it more effectively.

A sometimes difficult means of acquiring knowledge is using the trial and error method. Trial and error can be painstaking, at times, but can be extremely valuable to you. Don't be afraid to make attempts in your life, even if they are sometimes bold maneuvers. Trial and error may be a slower, less efficient way of acquiring knowledge but it is usually a very effective way to retain information and retain it once you acquire it.

Formal Education

Naturally, a primary way to acquire knowledge is through formal education. Applying yourself in school is a commitment that you need to make, and instill in your children, if you have any. Continuing your education, either by seeking terminal degrees or merely taking classes, is a good idea throughout your life. Although learning is more difficult in the geriatric brain, it exercises the neural pathways keeping them active and the brain young. Education is knowledge and knowledge is freedom. The type of freedom that allows you to think the way you want without limitations of ignorance. Educating yourself throughout your life will help keep your freedom. Whether you do so through formal adult education classes, formal academic degrees, or by reading and talking to learned individuals, expanding your mind with information will help you think, analyze, and solve problems with great decision making skills.

Informal Education

Acquiring knowledge is not restricted to what you learn in a classroom. There are also, less evident ways you can accumulate knowledge in your life. One of them is to observe. As you go through your life and engage in different social, occupational, and cultural experiences, make sure you observe. Watch what is going on around you. Take specific notice of the impact you have on others. Learn from what you see and the information that is placed before you. Do not let events go unnoticed or unprocessed. Think about what is going on around you. Keep your eyes and ears alert to new information, even if it doesn't seem relevant at the time. Many people go through life passively, thereby missing important information to be learned and used. Oftentimes information does not have relevance in the moment, but can be useful at a

ACHIEVING FREEDOM PART I

later date or in a different situation. File away things you see in your memory so that you can apply those concepts when the appropriate moment arises. Many things you learn and file away do not seem to have relevance until they fit in a specific situation. That is the "aha" moment that gives the previously unimportant tidbit of information significant meaning.

Active Listening

Listening is another way to increase your knowledge to gain freedom. Listening feeds you information, understanding, provides enjoyment in your life, and learning. Not passive listening, actively listening to what people have to say. Active listening involves asking questions about what is said. It also involves interpreting, synthesizing, and scrutinizing information and not taking it at face value. Here is where your formal education and analytical thinking kick in. Active listening can help you in specific situations when you feel like a fish out of water. That is, you are in a novel situation and you don't know the appropriate way to act and what to say. Active listening, combined with good observation, will guide you through these situations. Active listening will also enable you to do that filing away of what seems to be unimportant information to be used at a later date when it can be appropriately applied.

Trial And Error

Learning by trial and error can be instrumental in gaining knowledge. Trial and error involves the willingness to fail. It also demands a certain amount of frustration tolerance because sometimes it takes more than one, or many trials before you are successful.

Trial and error learning requires patience. Patience is not about waiting and doing nothing. Patience is more about waiting for the right time to act or take advantage of the circumstances in a situation. Remaining in your comfort zone and not venturing out to try different experiences will stifle your learning and limit your knowledge. As mentioned earlier, trial and error learning can be painstakingly difficult. Tolerance of frustration, patience, and the willingness to make a mistake are all part of learning by trial and error. Parenting is a great example of trial and error learning. The only training for parenting is what you learned from how you were parented. There is no manual for how to be a good parent. There are plenty of parenting books but none that cover the intangible situations and issues parents encounter with their children. I once wrote an article entitled, "*I Was An Excellent Parent Until I Started Having Children.*" Trial and error is the on-the-job training that most good parents use to raise happy, well-adjusted kids.

Applying Knowledge

The most obvious application of your accumulated knowledge would be in your selected vocation. Knowledge enables you to be successful and productive regardless of what job you do. Accumulating as much knowledge as possible in your job will prove to be a priceless asset. It's probably a good idea to try to learn about other people's jobs, as well. Being able to think with accurate information and process it intelligently will undoubtedly increase your success at work. You can work more efficiently, streamline when you need to, problem solve, and develop new ideas or procedures to be more productive and score points with your boss. The knowledge you have gained in your formal education will only go so far. Whether it is a high school diploma, college or graduate degree, it is only a foundation to be utilized in your job. You must use listening, observing, and trial and error to truly be successful in your job.

The other venue to apply knowledge to gain freedom is in the social arena. Using knowledge in your social interactions helps you in several ways. Knowledge helps you identify your morals, apply your values, make appropriate judgments, and strengthens your social acumen.

With knowledge, you are free to decide what moral behavior is best for you. By best, I mean most consistent with your personality, values, and how they are helpful in pursuit of your happiness. Values are subjective and unique to each of us. Values cannot be defined by others, which means you need knowledge to decide on what is important to you. What do you value and why do you value it? There was a clever television commercial where a recent college graduate son was sitting at the kitchen table talking with his father. He tells his father that he just sold his car and emptied his bank account and wants to go cross country and tour for a few months. The father, astonished and seemingly upset, repeats his son's plans in an almost sarcastic tone of voice. The 50 something father pauses and then states, "I wish I had done that!" His son decided that traveling, being free, and experiencing the country was much more valuable to him at that point in his life as opposed to the traditional path of securing a job and entering his career path.

Knowledge helps you make good judgments and decisions in your life. It provides you with as much information as possible in order to make a high percentage good decision for yourself. Being able to weigh the alternatives because you are aware of the alternatives facilitates the decision making process. With enough good decisions under your belt, and learning how to actively listen and observe, you end up having good social acumen. Social acumen is intuitive. It is a natural way to react in social situations, using the knowledge you have acquired, to just seamlessly navigate through social situations and interpersonal relationships.

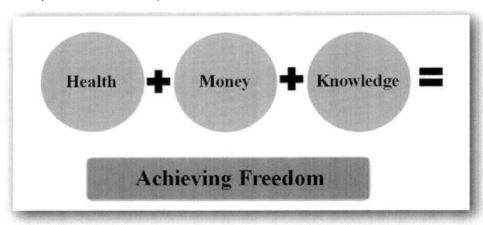

Freedom

Freedom is at the very core of securing happiness and self-fulfillment. To approach the notion of having as much freedom in your life as possible, you must embrace the trio of health, money, and knowledge as the fundamental components that will get you on your way to having as much freedom in your life as possible. Maintaining your physical and mental health sets you up to be available to manage anything that comes your way in life. Your health keeps you sharp, energetic, and motivated. Money, whether you consider it to be the root of all evil or the source of all pleasure, holds a great deal of importance because, realistically, you live in a capitalistic society. Money provides you with the means to acquire things you want and need. Money also enables you the freedom to seek adventure in your life, or simply do the things necessary to function on a high level. Knowledge helps you make sound decisions and provides you with the ability to think in a free manner. Knowledge removes the invisible boundaries that ignorance and rigid thinking construct in your own mind.

Maintaining *health*, using *money* in an appropriate manner, and acquiring *knowledge* is a basis for living a life filled with happiness, freedom, and self-fulfillment. Freedom, as it relates to your leading a happy life, enables you to take as much control over your life as possible. It gives you options, minimizes barriers and boundaries, and facilitates personal growth. Freedom gives you the opportunity to make the train if you chose to make the train. But with freedom, the train doesn't leave without you because you have the option as to whether or not you need to take that train. If you are knowledgeable about the train schedule, don't have any health limitations in riding trains, and have the money, you can take any train you want.

The Freedom Triad of health, money, and knowledge are mutually exclusive. That is, they are independent of one another. You can have great health but little money and minimal knowledge. Wealth can be a strength in your life but you may not have good health or adequate knowledge. You can be the most knowledgeable person in the world but not enjoy good health and have little money. Interestingly, they are connected in that each individual component can facilitate success in the other two components in the triad. In other words, they stand alone but one helps you achieve the other two. Despite the fact that they are mutually exclusive they need to be achieved both individually and simultaneously. Although this Freedom Triad is basic and essential in your life, merely having them does not provide you with freedom. How they are acquired and how you use them gives you the real satisfying life you are looking for. That is, the process of achieving health and acquiring money and knowledge always needs to be accomplished with integrity, ethically, and respectfully.

CHAPTER 4

Achieving Freedom- Part II

*Responsibility*Maturity*Self Discipline*

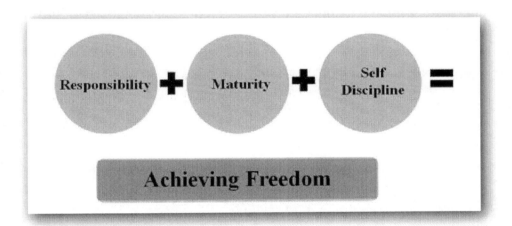

Responsibility

When it comes to freedom, responsibility, for many people, has a negative connotation. They may ask, "How can I be free when my life is filled with responsibilities?" Ironically, it is just the opposite. Sigmund Freud said,

"Most people do not really want freedom, because freedom involves responsibility, and most people are frightened of responsibility."

The negative attachment to the word "responsibility" has its roots in your childhood. When you were a child, responsibility was probably drummed into you on a regular basis, usually as a negative or reprimanding statement. Do any of these resounding statements remind you of your parents' talking? Or, maybe, it is you telling your own children.

"You have to be responsible for your things!"

"Where is your sense of responsibility?"

"This was *your* responsibility!"

"You are responsible for hurting your brother."

"Now that you are older, you have to be responsible for doing that on your own."

"Your homework is your responsibility; I already went through 8th grade."

Those messages were all associated with growing up issues, needing to be serious, and feeling criticized or inadequate in some way. These common parental statements usually related to tasks or actions that probably had no interest to you as a child. But, you are not a child anymore. It means that you are an adult and for some people, that is scary. Responsibilities may weigh heavily on your shoulders, you may resent having them, and they may be boring. Well, as an old coach of mine used to say, "Suck it up and play through the pain." Taking care of the responsibilities in your life is key to having freedom in your life. I believe that the more responsible you are, the more responsibilities you take care of efficiently and effectively, you will receive more freedom, privileges, choices, and niceties in your life.

Responsibility Is An Oxymoron

In some ways, responsibility is somewhat of an oxymoron. It seems like being responsible could be in direct competition with having freedom in your life. After all, if you are taking care of responsibilities you are spending your time attending to tasks that are usually not enjoyable or preferable. We already know that time is finite and if you use it up doing "the responsible thing" then that cuts into your discretionary time to spend on leisure and fun activities.

Another way responsibility is a contradiction lies in the root word, "response." Being responsible is not about responding or reacting. On the contrary, it is about being proactive, planful, and taking initiative. If you are responding and reacting to the demands of life, then you may be operating with undue stress, anxiety, and inefficiency. Responding creates limitations and boundaries for you because it forces you to attend to the demand in the moment instead of when you want to attend to it. Responding also implies that you are doing damage control in a situation that calls for your attention to repair something or attend to something immediately before it becomes a problem.

The Power of Responsibility
Despite the visceral negative feeling responsibility may carry with it, the more responsible you are in your life the more power and freedom you actually will have. Taking care of the basic responsibilities in your life establishes the foundation for a strong, secure life. Taking care of your responsibilities creates room for fluff and fun in your life. Responsibilities encompass everything from doing your laundry to filing your taxes and everything else in between. It means attending to and following through with educational or employment demands.

Meeting your responsibilities simply takes care of all of the minutia and basic functions in your life. It provides a strong foundation that eventually affords you the ability to enjoy activities and opportunities that may not be available if you are irresponsible. Everything in your life falls into one of two categories. The first category includes things you have to do even though you may not particularly enjoy or want to do them. The second category includes things you want to do, things that are enjoyable to do. The trick is to make sure you take care all of the things you *have* to do. If you are attending to the *have to's* then you end up getting more and more of the *want to's*. In fact, if you are really responsible, you increase the chances that *have to's* and *want to's* end up being the same thing. I need to work to support my family financially, but the work that I do I love to do. I don't go to work or to my job, I just go to the office. It isn't work to me. Richard, a 27-year-old patient, is an excellent example of the benefit of the relationship between the things you have to do in your life and the things you want to do in your life.

Prioritizing Responsibilities

When Richard first came to see me he was riddled with stress and anxiety in his life. The source of his difficulties was quickly identified. Richard was employed as an assistant manager of a major chain pharmacy store. He also took two classes each semester, trying to complete his college degree. His chief complaint when he entered therapy was that he had little time or money to do the things he wanted to do with friends. He was perpetually late for work, frequently rallying the night before a big assignment was due, and behind in his bills on a regular basis, including the $2000 he borrowed from his parents to move into his apartment. He felt like his life was out of control and that he was constantly operating in catch up or crisis mode.

As we explored how he was managing, or more accurately, mismanaging his life we discovered that he was able to spend time on the things he liked to do. He loved playing a specific online video game, watching football on television, and hanging out with his friends. Richard constantly felt that he spent so much time working and going to school, that he had to spend time with his friends and doing the things he liked whenever he could. The problem was that he was actually "stealing" time from his school work and money from his bank account to be able to do so. I asked him to keep a log recording the dates and times he would engage in these preferred activities. He quickly discovered that he was late for work and classes because he played video games in the morning. He would often finish working, plan to study or complete a paper for school that night, but would get a call from a friend to watch Monday Night Football. This resulted in his staying up late to complete his schoolwork, causing him to be tired in the morning, and subsequently late for work-again. He would get his paycheck every other week, put it in his checking account and access it using his debit card. Richard had fixed monthly bills, most associated with his rental apartment, as well as $50 a month to repay his parents, gas for his car, and credit card debt. At the end of the month he would find himself short of cash, creating a great amount of stress for Richard. He has yet to give his parents a monthly check as an agreed schedule to repay the money they lent him. Instead of going food shopping, he would either go out for meals or order food in.

Richard exhibited a clear and consistent pattern of putting off his time, financial, and academic responsibilities behind the things he wanted to do. In other words, he would perpetually put his *want to's* ahead of his *have to's*. He needed a structure in place so that he could make sure he took care of his responsibilities first.

We decided that every Sunday night he would establish a schedule, first placing the fixed time commitments such as his work schedule, his class schedule, and any other scheduled appointments. Next, he placed specific blocks of time for study and homework throughout the week. He also scheduled a trip to the supermarket so he could have food in his apartment instead of eating every meal from a restaurant. We also had Richard open a savings account and direct deposit his paycheck into it. He established a budget to determine his fixed monthly expenses plus a small amount to go for savings and subtracted that from his take-home pay. The remainder was his fun money. Now when he was paid, he would transfer only that amount to his checking account so that he would only have access to it. The savings account money was only used to pay bills when they were due, including his monthly payback to his parents.

Basically, Richard had to learn to first and foremost, take care of the things he is responsible before he can play. He was running his life inversely creating time and financial stress and crisis. There was never enough time or money to meet his expenses, job, and academic demands. Once he corrected the order of things, he actually discovered that he had more time and money and that he was enjoying his life much more. Sure, there were periods of time when he had little money or time, such as at the end of the month and during exam time. But, he learned to accept this and focused on the benefits of taking care of his responsibilities more effectively and efficiently. Richard no longer felt cheated due to an inordinate amount of time spent working and going to school. His new sense of control over his life further motivated him to stick to his schedule and budget, making it easier for him to say "no" to the "*want to's*" when he needed to attend to the "*have to's.*"

Work now, play later

The strategy you need to employ, as Richard quickly learned, is to take care of your responsibilities now, so you can play later. This concept is especially more difficult in our present culture, where there is a high emphasis on self-gratification and 24/7 distraction with technological devices offering social media, instantaneous contact with friends from wherever you are and whenever you want, and Internet based entertainment. I have a chapter in my book, *Generation Text: Raising Well Adjusted Kids In An Age Of Instant Everything*" entitled "Work Now, Play Later." I originally had it titled, "Play Now, Play Later" but my publisher thought it was too negative. However, this is how many people, like Richard, run their lives. Despite the fact that most adults had "work now, play later" drummed into them as a child, they still seek the pleasure first and try to fit the chores in later. The problem is that there is often limited or even no time to take care of the responsibilities if you wait until you are finished with what you *want* to do.

Promptly attending to your responsibilities and fulfilling them on an ongoing basis means paying close attention to the details of that responsibility. No matter how seemingly insignificant or life impacting your responsibilities are, do them promptly, thoroughly, and completely. Being responsible is closely tied to your work ethic, which will be expounded upon in Chapter Eight entitled "Work Ethic."

Sense of Responsibility

The underlying factor in being responsible is having a sense of responsibility. That means it is just a part of you that naturally looks for, attends to, and takes on responsibility in your life. It is a commitment that is ingrained and taking care of your responsibilities is very natural to you. Being responsible needs to be part of your identity so you automatically, almost without thinking, complete the tasks and chores that run your life smoothly. If you think about it, you can easily identify what those tasks are because you know very well what happens if you procrastinate or neglect the daily functions in life. And it's not just the relatively small, daily chores. You need to attend to those social, vocational, and relationship responsibilities, as well. Having a sense of responsibility comes from a firm commitment to yourself and others that you will meet all the demands that life throws your way. Shirking responsibility only diminishes your freedom, limits your choices made available to you in life, and makes you face bigger and graver responsibilities in the future. Your train will keep leaving without you.

Maturity

Maturity is the second dimension in the *Responsibility/Maturity/Self Discipline* paradigm to obtaining freedom in your life. Acting maturely and being responsible are closely connected concepts. The major difference between the two is that acting responsible is totally and completely within your power and ability as long as the expectations are reasonable. Maturity, on the other hand, has a bilateral aspect to it. Maturity is two-sided. One aspect of maturity is biologically driven, as determined and defined by the individual's developmental age. The other aspect is associated with conscious choices in specific situations. These choices are within your skill set and capabilities that you already have mastery over.

Developmental Maturity

You can only act as maturely as your biology and developmental stage of life will permit. In this sense, maturity is associated with human development and what is expected of you at the time of your specific age. For example, a 15-year-old would not be expected to handle a romantic relationship with another 15-year-old the same way a 35-year-old would with another 35- year-old. The expectation for the teenager would be commensurate with that developmental age. We can only expect that much given the limitations of his life experiences, social, cognitive, and emotional development at that point in his life. There are developmental limitations and capacities even in adulthood. A 32-year-old, first year United States Senator is not going to function at the same maturity level as a four term, 59-year-old senior Senator.

Acting in a mature manner really means acting your age. I remember reprimanding my son's behavior when he was a toddler. Realizing that he really couldn't help himself, at the end of my correcting his behavior I quipped, "You are acting like a 4-year-old." To which he intelligently responded, "But Daddy, I am a 4-year-old!" In other words, his behavior was commensurate with his maturity level. So the first lesson is, try to act your age and only have expectations for others that are consistent with their developmental capabilities.

Maturity Is Sometimes A Choice

Acting in a mature manner to secure your quest for freedom is often volitional. If you are in tune to your behavior and the situation you are in at the time, you can monitor and regulate your actions to that you act as maturely as you possibly can. One way to accomplish mature behavior is to observe and take notice of how most people are behaving, especially if they are older or more experienced than you.

Anthony, a 34-year-old software salesman expressed some anxiety about attending his first regional sales meeting. He had been working in the main office of the company processing orders for 4 years and was recently promoted to the sales position. The regional sales manager was notorious for calling people out in meetings, and having them respond to questions or present their thoughts on the topic at hand. Anthony was extremely nervous, as he never attended a meeting such as this, and was afraid that he wouldn't know what to do if he was called on. I told him to watch and listen to how the more seasoned salespeople handled it. Do they stand up when they speak? Notice their nonverbal behavior in terms of eye contact, to whom they address their answers, and their volume and tone of voice when they speak. Take note of how they handle a question to which they don't know the answer.

Governing your behavior and making sure it is appropriate for the situation is a way to choose to act maturely. Understanding that the same behaviors can be appropriate in one setting, yet inappropriate in others is also acting maturely. For example, if you are at a baseball game and the home team scores a run, you and most of the crowd at the stadium stand up, yell, cheer, scream, clap your hands, and high five one another. This is appropriate behavior for that situation in that setting. But if you are at a PGA tournament and a golfer you root for drives the ball right onto the green, I hardly think that you would yell, scream, clap your hands, and high-five the guy standing next to you. Maturity involves recognizing that those same behaviors would be inappropriate for that setting.

Emotional Maturity

Emotional maturity entails regulating your emotions so that they are appropriate for the situation. Expressing your feelings in an extreme manner, whether it be elation, sadness, disappointment, or anger, will come across as immature and make others feel uncomfortable. I am not suggesting that you present yourself as a robot, but I do think that managing your feelings within a temperate range of expression will come across as mature. Maturity is tantamount to exhibiting self-control. When you have self-control, you will position yourself to be able to think rationally, and deal with situations and people in a reasonable manner.

Regulating your emotional responses as a way to present yourself as mature usually results in people perceiving you as stable and even tempered. Consequently, others will place a lot of faith and trust in your opinions. Consequently, it puts you in a place that gives you credibility enabling you to have a meaningful impact on individuals and groups.

Social Maturity

Being socially mature enables you to not only increase the potential for successful interpersonal relationships, it also helps you be accepted by others on a higher and more sophisticated level with more credibility. You will always be accepted at the level you present yourself. If you come across as lacking self-confidence, unsure, impulsive, and immature, you will be accepted at that lower level. If you come across as confident, thoughtful, and with strong conviction, you will command respect and be accepted at a very high level. Social maturity is as much a state of mind as it is a set of behaviors when you are with others.

Even if you are not completely confident in a specific situation you should try to be like a "duck on water." Picture a duck ever so slowly gliding across a serene, gentle pond. It floats quietly and self-assured in a peaceful, almost melodic manner. But underneath, what you don't see, is its feet paddling voraciously and violently to keep it in motion. It is that frantic, I'm not sure I know what I am doing part of you that should remain submerged so that people only see a calm, self-assured individual. That is not to say that you should be cocky or act over confident. People see through that very quickly.

Immaturity

Immaturity can be a problem in so many ways. If you act immaturely, you will not be afforded privileges and opportunities. Others will lack confidence in you, not give you the benefit of the doubt, and not offer you opportunities even if your skill set is capable of meeting with success. It is important to take a look at yourself and assess your level of maturity in terms of your behavior, expression of your feelings, and how you interact socially. Immaturity will limit your freedom because it closes doors of opportunity, limits choices, and restricts your access to privileges. Others will simply believe that you just can't handle freedom due to immature behavior.

Jon is a 20-year-old who lives with his parents and commutes to a local community college. He often complains in therapy sessions about how his parents still see him as a child because they treat him as such. Jon cites many examples of this such as the fact that he has a 1:00 AM curfew, they are constantly nagging him about his school work, and they frequently offer "coaching" when it comes to his friendships.

I suggested that we have a session with Jon's parents so that we can confront the issue straight on. Jon reluctantly agreed and the following week his parents accompanied him to the appointment. As it turned out, Jon's parents were actually resentful that they had to impose restrictions on Jon and had to frequently address inappropriate behavior they witnessed with his peers. They also did not want to even be remotely involved in his homework and keeping track of when his exams were to make sure he studied. To Jon's surprise, his parents wanted the same thing he wanted-to be treated like a 20-year-old. "So, why do you feel the need to help Jon?" I asked. His mother immediately went into a diatribe; jumping at the chance to reveal to me Jon's overall functioning.

"Jon consistently comes in late during the week, often missing classes or has difficulty waking up for morning classes. On weekends, he was staying out to the wee hours of the morning, and then loses all day Saturday and Sunday due to sleep which affects his study time. Often, he does not do assignments, forgets to do them, or is trying to complete a 5-page paper that he starts the night before it is due. He plays video games when he is home, sometimes until very late at night. Jon has failed classes and received "D's" in others. We see how he is with his friends. He seems to have no filters, saying whatever comes out of his mouth. He thinks it is funny to shoot digs out to his friends and we see him sometimes trying to roughhouse with them. He also makes inappropriate, immature jokes about girls and sex. When his friends ask him to stop, he doesn't. We see his friends pulling away from him because he acts like he is in middle school, not college. Jon is beginning to see that his friends are just tolerating him, and they will not call him to do go out, but they let him come with them when he calls them.

It quickly became apparent why Jon's parents were treating him as if he was a young child. It was because he was acting like one. His behavior and attitude presented on the level of a much younger child so they felt the need to treat him with limits and boundaries due to the fact that he was not mature enough to impose them on himself. They felt the need to coach him on his social skills because he wasn't acting like a typical college student and they saw him jeopardizing his friendships. Basically, his immature behavior resulted in a loss of respect, confidence, freedom, privileges, and perhaps even his friends.

Self-Discipline

Freedom does not usually come for free. As you read through the sections on *Responsibility* and *Maturity* it should become clear to you that there can be a great deal of sacrifice associated with obtaining freedom. That sacrifice, or sometimes self-denial, involves a certain amount of self-discipline. Self-Discipline is the third dimension in the triad for leading a life filled with freedom, happiness, and self-fulfillment.

Self-discipline is tantamount to self-control. You, and only you, have the power over yourself. The train will not leave without you if you exercise self-control and self-discipline. Denying yourself, at the right time, in the right situation, involves controlling your impulses, delaying or denying momentary gratification, and, once again, discriminating between work time and play time.

Impulse Control

Impulse control is simply thinking before you act. Poor impulse control is acting without thought, or acting before you think. There is a certain degree of neuro-biology that determines how well you control your impulses. As a young child your brain did not have the ability to exercise self-discipline and self-control because the central nervous system was immature and not yet developed. As you got older, the neuro-pathways became better established and you developed the ability to control your impulses. This is the beginnings of self-discipline.

I believe that we walk around every day experiencing dozens, maybe even hundreds of impulses that are automatically repressed. They are not within our awareness but our brains have been trained to instantaneously squelch emerging impulses. These automatic impulses occurring subconsciously are not of concern to us. Impulses that enter our awareness tempt us, usually drive us toward un-healthy, negative, or even dangerous actions. These are the impulses that beg us to implement self-discipline. These are the impulses that can interfere with our quest for freedom and leading a healthy life. Unfortunately, these impulses are also quite difficult to corral. They can range from seeing a piece of apple pie in the refrigera-tor when you are on a diet to stopping yourself from gambling or drinking.

Your Impulses

Everyone has to deal with impulses but everyone's impulse vulnerabilities are not the same. Some people have no problem controlling gambling or dieting and some people are addicted to gambling and have over-eating disorders. Some people can keep their hands off of a colleague when engaged in a con-versation, and some people cannot stop themselves from touching their arm or hand when conversing.

What are the impulses that you struggle with? It is important to first, iden-tify your Achilles heel weaknesses. Once you are acutely aware of your impulse weaknesses, you can begin to consciously attempt to control them using self-discipline. The idea is to disrupt or interfere with the impulse to act by taking the time to think it through. Thinking it through entails emphasizing the conse-quences of following through with the action, and reminding yourself how you will feel if you eat that piece of pie. You will need to do this "self-talk" repeatedly, and then create a detour for the impulse by redirecting your focus on another activity. Thomas, a 34-year-old patient, was having difficulty with self-discipline due to a popular online video game called StarCraft. StarCraft became a problem for Thomas because it created a constant rift with his wife, and it pulled him away from other responsibilities. Thomas had difficulty controlling his impulse to play the game every time he needed to open his computer whether it was for work related tasks or doing his online banking. One way to deal with persistent negative impulses is to eliminate them from your life. If alcohol is your impulse problem, do not have any in your home, do not go into bars, and do not spend time with people who include alcohol as an important part of their life. If you are on a diet, do not work in a bakery. The problem with an impulse like Thomas' is that you can't avoid the computer. It has become a necessary part of our lives and is unavoidable. So, he needed to exercise self-discipline every time he opened his computer, which could be several times a day.

Once Thomas accepted and surrendered to the fact that StarCraft was a problem in his life we created an internal script to combat the need to play it. That script emphasized the consequences of playing in that moment. They included not getting his report for work done on time and dealing with his boss, dealing with the wrath of his wife as she complained about his constantly playing "that game," and the guilty, anxious feeling he experiences after he finishes playing. In this situation, Thomas was unable to redirect his attention on something else because he needed to be on the computer to do his work. So he had to force himself to begin his work task and hyper focus on it. He was also able to disengage the game so that it would take extra steps to open it and play. The idea was to provide interference for the negative impulse so that practical, reasonable thoughts would prevail.

Delaying and Denying Gratification

Incorporated in having self-discipline is the concept of delaying and denying gratification. We all have wants and needs that provide us with a good feeling. Gratification takes the form of pleasurable activities, physical objects, emotions, and sensory input. Acquiring material objects, for many people, strokes that gratification muscle. It can be buying new clothing, getting a new car, or purchasing knick-knacks for your home. The need for emotional gratification is satisfied by engaging in social interactions that gives you a good feeling inside. Sometimes that feeling is stronger and moves into the elation realm. Sensory gratification has to do with tactile, or good feelings associated with auditory, visual, olfactory, or taste. Eating, drinking, and sex commonly fall into these categories.

Gratification gives you an endorphin rush and can be quite powerful. You need to employ delaying gratification when the timing is not appropriate or helpful. Unfortunately, there are also many instances when you must actually deny yourself gratification because it is inappropriate or even harmful. You must say "no" even when you really want to say "yes" to yourself. Exercising self-discipline when it comes to delaying and denying gratification can be quite difficult, but will eventually lead to a lifestyle that you are in charge of. Running your life, or making the train, will minimize crisis and help keep you healthy and successful. Exercising self-discipline, in concert with responsibility and maturity, will help lead you to a lifestyle filled with freedom, self-fulfillment, and happiness.

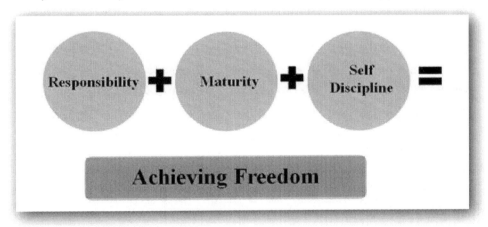

Freedom
Having a "free" feeling as you go through your life is such a key to happiness that it warrants two chapters in this book. In addition to the triad of *Health/*

Money/Knowledge, the magic number "3" that leads to freedom also entails the combination of Responsibility, Maturity, and Self Discipline.

The Health/Money/Knowledge triad are a means to help you obtain as much freedom in your life as possible. Responsibility, Maturity, and Self Discipline are more of an action that you take or self-impose in order to obtain as much freedom in your life as possible.

Acting in a responsible and mature manner while using self-regulation and self-discipline, will position you to be the beneficiary of privileges and freedoms that would otherwise not be offered to you by others. You will be respected and trusted so that you can manage the freedom in a responsible way. Obtaining a driver's license at the legal age your state allows is a concrete example of how acting responsibly, maturely, and with self-discipline entitles you to the freedom of driving. In many states the legal driving age is seventeen. When a person reaches their seventeenth birthday and they meet the requirements to obtain a legal driver's license, they acquire the privilege and freedom to drive an automobile. However, if they get a few speeding tickets, drive recklessly, play "games" with the car like chicken or drag racing, and have even a minor accident or two, either the state or the parents take away the privilege of driving. Acting irresponsibly, immaturely, and lacking self-discipline results in losing the freedom to drive a car. Conversely, driving responsibly, obeying the traffic laws, and regulating impulses to speed or play games with the car will result in maintaining the privilege and freedom of driving.

CHAPTER 5

Relationships

*Honesty*Love and Caring*Respect*

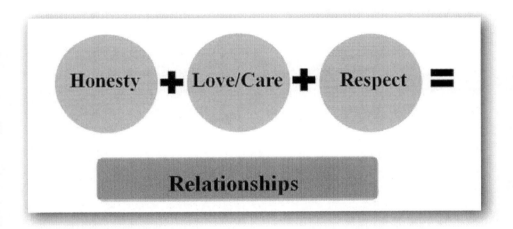

Honesty

Honesty is at the core of building trust in relationships. I believe that couples that are committed to each other for the long-haul should be able to be completely honest with one another about any topic. You should be able to discuss everything from sexual issues to how a particular article of clothing looks on your romantic partner without fear of an angry or defensive reaction. Sensitive issues need to be addressed in a sensitive manner, and delivered with care and avoiding a critical, attacking posture. If you have an open, honest relationship, you can trust each other with your inner most thoughts, feelings, and secrets without concern for ridicule or having the information used against you in the future. That is not to say that you should be dishonest with a person you just started dating or with someone with whom you are casually dating. The stage of development in these types of relationships does not call for the same kind of openness and honesty about feelings, thoughts, and secrets, as compared to a long-term committed relationship. The distinction is that you need to be honest in your more casual dating and noncommittal relationships, but not as self-disclosing until the trust has been consistently established.

Honesty among friends and relatives has a slightly different twist. There are certain boundaries among friends and relatives that are not present in your committed romantic relationships. Still, as in casual dating relationships, honesty must prevail, with caution to how open you are with your inner thoughts and feelings. Being sensitive to your friend's or sister's feelings should take priority over completely open comments and criticisms of him or her.

Being honest means avoiding deception and sneakiness in your relationships. Also to be avoided are lies of omission, as will be discussed in the next section. Telling only a half truth and leaving out important aspects is tantamount to lying. It leads the listener to assumptions that will undoubtedly be erroneous. Being forthright, above board, and honest will solidify your relationships because it will facilitate trust.

Dishonesty

There are two forms of dishonesty. The first, which is the most obvious, is outright lying. When you lie about something, you usually have to create more lies because of the first lie. I had a patient tell me that about fifteen years ago when she first moved to the town she presently lives in, she lied about her age by 4 years. Now that she and her friends are reaching milestone birthdays, she has to lie to her friends, while her family celebrates her true 50th birthday. She could not invite her closest friends to a dinner party her husband arranged for her and had to lie to her family as to why they weren't invited. She also had to lie about how long she was married because otherwise it wouldn't jive with her age because her friends knew how old she was when she got married. She experienced a constant anxiety when her sister was included in social events with her friends. She would be so embarrassed if the subject of her age came up because she would be found out. People who lie eventually get caught in lies. Once this occurs, it damages the relationship, and prevents it from becoming closer. Trust is jeopardized.

A second form of lying is the lie of omission. A lie of omission is when you lead the person to a misperception or misrepresentation by leaving out an important part of an event. A lie of omission can also take the form of allowing the person to continue believing something about the event even though you know it isn't true. Lies of omission are partial truths that perpetuate deception in order to protect you in some way.

When your boss asks you for the monthly report that was due a week ago, you respond, "I am waiting for Joe to give me last month's data I need to complete the report." That happens to be the truth, but it is only the partial truth because the part you aren't telling your boss is that you didn't ask Joe to give you that piece until the day before the report was due. Next thing you know, your boss happens to run into Joe in the coffee shop down the street from your office and he asks him about it. Eventually, this type of lie catches up to you and you lose integrity and trust with your boss.

Children will often present lies of omission. Jaime, an 11-year-old patient was feeling very sad because she told me no one likes to play with her during recess and the kids didn't like her. Even when she asked to be included in playground games they refused to let her play. Appearing like a true victim, Jaime was leaving out important parts of the playground story. She failed to inform me that she will try to cheat during games, argue when she is called "out," and is not a gracious winner when she does win a game.

Lying and deception create tremendous distrust in your relationships and should be avoided at all times. Trust has such a strong influence over the quality of your relationships yet is so tenuous. You can be trustworthy and trusted for years, get caught in a lie and it is almost as if you are starting at square one with trust in that relationship. If you get caught in lies or deception it takes a long time to recapture your trust with that individual.

Love/Care

It is not unique that the qualities of the triad *honesty, love*/care, and respect are needed to accomplish the goal; in this case a happy, healthy relationship. The goals of most of the other triads also require all three, but for a healthy relationship it is essential that all three are strong. If one of the three is weak, it cannot be a healthy relationship. For example, the previous chapter addressed the issue of freedom in your life by developing responsibility, maturity, and self-discipline. If you are strong in responsibility and self-discipline, but weaker in maturity, you can still achieve freedom. If your responsibility is weaker but you are strong in maturity and self-discipline, they will compensate for the weaker of the trio and still afford you freedom and privileges. It is more difficult if one is weaker, but still attainable.

The uniqueness about the *honesty/love and caring/respect* triad is that you cannot sustain a healthy relationship if any one of the three is weak. All three dimensions need to be strong and evident within the relationship in order for it to be sustained as a healthy relationship. Even though all three dimensions are required for a healthy relationship, the loving and caring aspect of the relationship triad happens to be a bit more critical, even essential, than the honesty and respect pieces. If the relationship is a romantic one, then there must be love and it must be strong. Loving is not enough, though, because in addition to love, basic caring must be part of the daily interaction as well. In all other relationships, basic care for one another must be present for the relationship to be strong and healthy.

Love Can Be A Tricky Word

"Love" is sometimes a tricky word to interpret. People say:

"I *love* hamburgers."
"I *loved* that movie."
"I *love* making *love.*"
"That is a *lovely* couch."
"I *love* to play games."
"You are a *love* for doing that for me."

And then there is, "I *love* to have a hamburger while watching a movie that I *love*, and then make *love* on a *lovely* couch, playing sexual games that I *love*, and my husband is a *love* for doing that for me." In other words, the word *love* is overused. So what kind of love are we actually referring to? Love should not be taken lightly. But for the purposes of our discussion, we refer to love as a strong, passionate feeling of affection for another person. There are different types of love depending on the nature of the relationship; family, friend, professional, or romantic partner. On a continuum, love would be far more intense and intimate than liking someone, or being fond of someone.

I once had a patient who frequently questioned herself as to whether or not she actually loved her husband. She thought she did, but she would compare it to the love she had for her son. For her son, she stated, she would not think twice about stepping in front of a bullet or an on-coming car to give up her life for his life. She wasn't sure if she would do that for her husband which created the question of love in her mind. It is difficult to measure love this way, because the nature of loving relationships is different.

Love takes many forms and has different levels of intensity in terms of passion and feelings. Caring, or having care for another person is part of loving, but you can certainly care about someone without loving them. The concept of love and care must be an essential part of healthy relationships regardless of the level of interpersonal connection; regardless of the nature of the relationship; and regardless of the status of the relationship. Whether it is a life partner, a sibling, friend, co-worker, or employee, you must have basic care or love (depending on that specific relationship) in order for it to be healthy, trusting, and contributory in a positive way for both of you.

Expression of Love/Care

If there is basic care or even love present in your relationship(s), it will not matter unless it is expressed in a way that the other person feels it. Both verbal and nonverbal communications are the most important and obvious ways love/care is expressed. Using words to express your feelings of admiration toward others, your adoration, love, and how important they are to you provide the glue for that relationship. Endearing words, words of appreciation, and words of gratitude need to be expressed intermittently and timely. Nonverbal communications such as hugs, holding hands, putting your arm around him or her, and smiling when you greet them are examples of how love and caring is expressed.

Expression of love/care is not exclusively demonstrated using verbal and nonverbal communications. Performing good deeds; small and large, miniscule and magnanimous, is another way to express love/care in your relationships.

Sometimes it is the little things that you do that communicate love and care. The following are examples of small, almost effortless gestures that go a long, long way in communicating love and care in your relationships.

- "You seem to be having a stressful week. What can I do to help make things a bit easier for you this week?" You recognize that he is going through a hard time and you offer to lighten his load in some way.
- Bring her coffee to her in bed one morning (or every morning). Small gestures like this go a long way in the "someone should pamper you" department.
- Offer to carry things if you see he has his hands filled with packages.
- In general, adopt the attitude, "What can I do to make your life easier?" Without insulting the person's sense of independence, if you frequently offer to do things that just make your friend or lover's life a bit easier, it demonstrates a great deal of caring.
- Give him a hug (when it is appropriate for the relationship) just because.
- Text or call during the work week with a funny anecdote or just to see how her day is going. This communicates that you think of the person even when you are not together. It communicates, "You are important to me."
- Listen attentively to the little things she likes and make it a point to pick it up for her. For example, if you are in a store and you happen

THE TRAIN KEEPS LEAVING WITHOUT ME

to see a specific difficult to find Asian Peanut salad dressing that she mentioned she liked, buy it for her. It will cost you $3.00 but will gain a great deal of points in the "care" department. You listened to her and acted on it.

- Without prompting, compliment his appearance. Notice if he lost weight. This needs to be done only if it is appropriate for the relationship. Generally, keep these comments out of the work place.
- Use well-mannered language. Listen to what your mother taught you. Always say "Thank you" and "please."

Some of the more magnanimous gestures also need to be present in your relationships in order to convey love and care. These require more time, effort, attention, and quite often, money.

- Remembering and recognizing birthdays, anniversaries, and other special occasions.
- Showing affection and physical warmth when the relationship is romantic in nature.
- Being considerate of one another.
- Showing support with time, attention, and good listening during difficult times.
- Initiating sex when the relationship is romantic in nature.
- Spending distraction free, screen free time together.
- Sharing your thoughts, feelings, and the events of your day, and expressing a sincere interest in his day.
- Initiating contact to get together or just to say, "How are you?"

All of the above gestures are expressed with behavior, actions, and verbal communication. Words are wonderful but they must be supported by actions. Letting a person know how important they are to you is an empty message unless you back it up with small and large gestures, consistently and frequently expressed. All of them demonstrate love and caring.

Respect

Having respect for one another in relationships entails respect and regard for each other's feelings, bodies, time, and possessions. Being respectful conveys a multitude of positive messages as well as helps create that ultimate trust that is needed for healthy relationships to exist. When you fully respect someone you are communicating to them an element of worthiness in that individual. With mutual respect both of you are communicating that you each have value and importance. Mutual respect yields a level playing field in the relationship so that control, power, and dominance are minimized and equalized. Feeling like you need to be submissive or a second class citizen in the relationship occurs when there is a lack of respect. Control, power, and dominance in relationships are generally negative aspects in the relationship that end up weakening the honesty and love/care dimensions. Being respectful creates mutual regard and avoids a parent/child flavor to the relationship. Lack of respect taints your relationships in a very negative way, and will have a pervasive effect on the overall healthiness of the relationship.

Disrespect can be overt and blatant, such as physical abuse and name-calling. But it also occurs in more subtle forms, such as tone of voice, volume, sarcasm, dismissiveness, and disregard. These types of disrespect are more subliminal and are often extremely destructive over time. They become normal ways of treating one another and slowly erode the relationship into a very unhealthy one.

How Respect Affects Relationships

My psychological practice is located in an affluent area, where the socioeconomic status of many of the families I treat are considered middle class, upper middle class, and upper class. Many of these families have the luxury of choosing their roles in the family in terms of stay at home parents vs. pursuing a career outside of the home. This often creates a respect issue within the marriage. Tony and Ellen are prime examples of what happens when there is a lack of respect. Their story is an all too familiar one among the couples I treat due to the nature of how they have structured their roles within the family. Their story highlights how a weakness in the respect component of the relationship can affect the Love/care and Honesty components. It also illustrates how the relationship deteriorates when respect is jeopardized.

Tony And Ellen

Tony and Ellen met during their junior year in college. They married 2 years after graduation and have been married for 22 years and have two sons, 20-years-old and 17-years-old. Tony is extremely successful, with a salary just tipping the 7 figure range. Ellen has been a stay-at-home mom, managing the home and being the primary caretaker for their children. At the time they entered marital therapy with me, the older son was away at college and the younger son was graduating high school and going off to college in the fall. They have prepared well both for retirement and college tuition for both children and have no financial concerns whatsoever. Two years ago Ellen decided to start her own business because her role at home has changed due to the ages of her kids. She opened up a small gift shop in the town they live in. This required start-up money, which was provided by Tony. The store actually lost money the first two years but it is now breaking even every month.

Tony, being the primary source of income for the family viewed his role as provider, and therefore, had the power to make all the decisions about how the money was spent for the family. He outwardly supported Ellen in her new business, both financially and emotionally, but would hold the fact that it costs them money against her during arguments, whether or not they were monetary disagreements. Tony believed that since he made the money, Ellen did not have much of a say in how it was spent. Tony bought an expensive sports car, and although he informed Ellen that he was going to buy it, it was not a discussion nor was it a joint decision. Yet, Ellen needed to check with Tony if she wanted to make purchases that cost $1000.00. Tony would often make demeaning comments about "that little business" Ellen started. Tony would also frequently criticize the way Ellen would do things around the house, or carefully scrutinize the credit card bill, confronting her on what he believed to be frivolous purchases. He once became angry over a $300 pair of shoes she bought, when he was wearing $600 shoes. To avoid confrontation and criticism, Ellen began hiding purchases and lying about how the store was doing. Over time, she began to feel like she had a parent-child relationship with her husband, having to ask permission to do things, buy things, and was constantly feeling like she was "not good enough."

Essentially, Tony had a double standard in the relationship that was conveyed as a devaluation and disrespect for Ellen. He treated Ellen as if she had lower status in their marriage based on their roles. Being a home-maker did not make any money and the money that Tony made provided a wonderful living for them. As Ellen began to feel increasingly more disrespected, she began to be dishonest with Tony. Furthermore, she stopped feeling attracted to him, which negatively affected their sex life. When they started marital therapy Ellen was even questioning as to whether or not she still loved Tony. She knows she did when they got married, but her self-worth had diminished over time and became a pressing issue as she tried to change her identity in her new stage of life.

Tony and Ellen had to first regain the mutual respect they did once have before they could repair the honesty and love aspects of their relationship. As Tony began to recognize how his philosophy about how their family was being run was flawed, he began to treat Ellen as an equal partner. Tony actually accepted this quite rapidly as I had pointed out to him that his priorities were in the wrong place. His own self-worth was entangled with his net-worth and that transcended into his marriage. He quickly saw that his priority should not be on money-he had plenty of that-but instead on making his wife happy and feel like they were a team.

Respect yourself

Respect in relationships does not need to be earned. It should just automatically be present without strings or contingencies. The funny thing about respect is that although it should not have to be earned in a relationship, it can be lost in a relationship, just as it was in Tony and Ellen's marriage. It is quite easy to lose respect for yourself once you are disrespected. Be careful not to fall into that trap in any of your relationships. Just because someone treats you a certain way, doesn't mean you have to buy into the disrespect. It also doesn't mean you deserve to be treated poorly. In order to regain respect, respect yourself first, then command respect from others. Confront those who do not treat your feelings, body, time, or possessions in a respectful manner. If disrespect continues, you need to evaluate the value of that relationship in your life. Respect is more important than being liked. Having self-respect and giving respect to others is paramount for healthy, successful relationships. The Governor of New Jersey, Chris Christie said, ". . . the greatest lesson that mom ever taught me though was . . . there would be times in your life when you have to choose between being loved and being respected . . . she said to always pick being respected." Portraying respectful behavior, however, does bring a certain amount of adoration.

Respecting Children

Everyone knows that children should respect their parents and all adults. I believe that parents and adults should also respect children. That should not be confused with elevating children to adult status with adult liberties, and should not be confused with empowering children to do and get what they want. Respecting children means that their bodies, feelings, time, and possessions need to be regarded with care. It means helping them feel that they are worthwhile, important, and listened to. So when they ask why they can't have a cookie, your answer should not be "because I said so." They deserve the respect of an explanation as to why they can't have a cookie, or go to their friend's house, or stay up late, or play one more video game, etc.

Respecting children still maintains your authority over them and will not empower them if it is done correctly. There is no doubt that there is a double standard between adults and kids. Adults (e.g. parents and teachers) are permitted to speak in a stern, firm voice if the youngster is not being cooperative. Kids are not permitted to speak to adults this way. If there is a rule in your house that food cannot be brought into the bedroom but you, as the parent, decide that it is okay for you to eat in your bedroom because you are more responsible, then showing respect to your child is to explain to them that there is a double standard and why you are allowed and he or she is not.

Respect Is Not Agreeing

I have a 54-year-old patient who persistently told me that her husband says she is disrespectful to him. Sharon was always confused by this because she didn't realize how she was being disrespectful. Additionally, knowing this patient for many years it was difficult for me to picture her as being disrespectful. However, I am not naïve to think that she may be treating her husband differently than she treats the rest of the world, which is with utmost respect and kindness. Eventually, I realized that we needed to define what her husband meant by her being disrespectful. After processing several examples, I realized that whenever she did not agree with something he was saying, or an outlook about a situation he had, he would tell her she was being disrespectful. Respect is not synonymous with agreement. The way you disagree with someone determines respect, not simply disagreeing with them. Sharing the same opinions is not always necessary, but being respectful is.

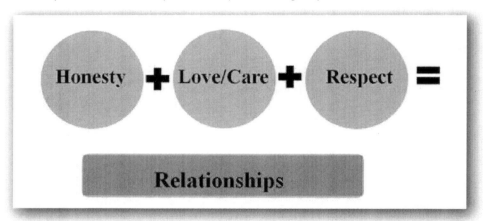

Relationships

Research indicates that people who have good social skills and satisfying relationships tend to have better self-esteem and lead happier lives. Having good relationships in your life doesn't necessarily mean having a lot of relationships, just healthy ones. Your romantic partner, if you have one, is the focal point and has the most impact on your overall happiness. Friends and extended family also add to your happiness. Psychologists have historically espoused the notion that only you are responsible for your own happiness. That no one can make you happy so do not place your happiness in another person's hands. I believe this to be only partially true. If you are not happy with yourself, then it will be difficult to be happy in your romantic partner and other relationships. However, where I differ from traditional thinking is that I believe that the quality of your romantic partner relationship can be the most significant factor in determining your happiness. Relationships do not define your happiness, but they do complement you, bring you to higher levels, and challenge you to be better. The converse can be true, as well. A bad relationship can taint your overall happiness no matter how successful, well liked, or how high your self-esteem.

Take 'Em Or Leave 'Em

Taking control of your life, a dominant theme in this book, is highly contingent upon terminating relationships that do not contribute positively in your life. Your investment of time and emotions should be made toward the relationships that do contribute positively to your happiness. Throughout this book I promote the fact that you almost always have choices in your life. Even when you believe you are trapped, you really are not. Naturally, there are exceptions, such as medical issues and physical limitations. With relationships, the reality is that you always have a choice with whom you include in your life. It is just that there are some relationships, such as with colleagues, family members, and bosses, that are less of a choice. Terminating these relationships usually results in significant consequences for choosing not to have them in your life. Nevertheless, there are always choices. That being said, let's place relationships into two general categories. We have relationships with people we choose and relationships we have with people with whom we are sort of stuck with in our lives. We could end those relationships but the stakes might be too high if we did, such as changing jobs when you love the work you are doing. Another example might be if you refuse to socialize with one particular individual, when he or she is part of your only social group who always includes him or her. You do have options in both of these examples but the consequences of eliminating them from your life may be worse than keeping them in your life.

The relationships you have in your life that positively contribute to your happiness need to be maintained. I do not mean "maintained" in the sense that you treat them in a maintenance mode. On the contrary, these relationships require persistent and consistent work in terms of attention, active involvement, and demonstration of care or love. These are the relationships that feed your inner emotional self, help you feel good about who you are, provide happiness, laughter, comfort, and sometimes, unconditional love. These are the people in your life that you consider to be important for whatever reason you deem their meaning or importance to you. You should make a list of all of the relationships you have in your life and evaluate them in terms of how or if they make you happy. Make it extensive and make notes on each individual. Surely, people on your list will bring some agita or negativity in your life so you will have to look at the whole picture when it comes down to evaluating their significance to your happiness.

Once you have identified and pensively assessed those relationships that are interfering or detracting from your happiness, try to determine if the issues can be ameliorated. That may mean confronting them, or not allowing you to be manipulated by them. This may be uncomfortable or cause friction, but if the relationship is worth saving, I support working on it-especially if it is your marriage. If they rank a complete zero in your life, or the issues cannot be resolved, get rid of them. If there is no hope or desire to improve these relationships, they are probably not worth saving. Holding onto them just because of longevity, happiness, or convenience will not serve you well. This may seem harsh in some cases, but it is all about you calling the shots in your life, and in this case, not letting the train telling you when to leave.

Maintaining Boundaries

If you are unwilling, or unable to terminate a specific relationship in your life because of the substantial consequences, then you must maintain boundaries within that relationship. These relationships are the people that are involuntarily inserted into our lives, such as a boss, co-worker, or the friend situation mentioned previously. There are also some people in your life that actually have redeeming qualities, but also have substantial negative impact on your happiness. There are aspects about them that you like and enjoy, but they also possess unpleasant qualities. For example, I have a 27-year-old patient, Brad, who has a friend that is fanatical about sports-a passion they both enjoy immensely. They attend sporting events together, talk sports, and play sports together. However, my patient abhors the way his friend Jason treats his girlfriends and women in general. So, he restricts his relationship with Jason to sports and will not go to parties with him. When Jason starts making disparaging or mocking comments about women, Brad quickly changes the subject. Establishing and maintaining boundaries with involuntary and so-so relationships will, at the very least, minimize the negative impact they have on you. It will allow you to include them in your life, enjoy the positive aspects of the relationship while minimizing the negative features.

Honesty*Love/Care*Respect

As stated earlier, the triad of *honesty, love/care, and respect* is somewhat unique in that I believe that it is impossible to have a healthy relationship with even one of these components missing or being a weakness in the relationship. Most of the other triads can accomplish the overall goal if one is weaker. But that is not the case with regard to having healthy relationships. They require all three aspects to be strong, and they apply to every relationship, regardless of the level of closeness or intimacy. The idea of requiring all three components for that relationship to be successful applies to the most loosely defined relationships all the way up to the closest, most intimate relationships.

When there is an honest, loving or caring relationship, and there is mutual respect, there will be a tremendous amount of trust. Trust is at the core of every relationship and without trust it cannot be a healthy relationship. When couples enter therapy with me I try to quickly assess the levels of honesty, love, and respect. Once the weak or missing dimensions are identified, we find ways to improve them. Invariably, one or more of them is weak or nonexistent, which is the underlying problem in their relationship. The following is a rather extreme example how unhealthy a relationship can be if one is missing, even when the other two are very strong.

Marc and Hope had been married for 7 years when they first consulted with me. Marc is an engineer and Hope is a pre-school teacher. They enjoyed a 4-year courtship prior to getting married and all was going well until recently. They both expressed their deep love for one another and a deep commitment to the marriage. Generally, they have felt happy together until Marc started exhibiting outbursts of anger, seemingly over small, inconsequential issues such as messiness in the home or Hope not being ready on time for social engagements. The work stress was clearly being displaced onto Hope and it soon evolved from verbal tirades to Marc becoming physically aggressive with Hope. His abuse was always followed by sincere apology and regret, as well as a promise to never do it again.

The couple expressed deep love for one another. They were also completely honest with one another, sharing all of the aspects of their life together as well as when they spent time at work or with friends. Their love and their honesty were solid. It was the respect part that was gone. Of course, Marc abusing Hope was completely inappropriate and disrespectful. But it goes well beyond that in the relationship. Hope began to have a "walking on egg-shells" feeling with Marc. She began to feel anxious, not knowing when the next blowup was coming. She began to feel afraid and started hiding things from him because she thought it might incite him. If it went on any longer, she would most likely stop loving him.

Despite the fact that this couple loved one another and was honest with one another, the respect dimension was extremely damaged. Over time, the love and honesty deteriorates due to the flaw in the respect realm. Fortunately, they sought help before it got to that point. Marc was sent for individual therapy to learn how to cope with his work stress and manage his anger more appropriately. The couple continued with me and we strengthened the mutual respect, and reinforced their love and honesty toward one another.

The triad of *honesty, love/care, and respect* is central to even the most loosely defined relationships. For example, when you go to the supermarket and go up to the cash register to pay for your merchandise, that interaction between you and the cashier can be loosely defined as a relationship. It is a short-lived, insignificant relationship in your life unless you instantly fall in love with the cashier and start dating. Other than that, the only goal in this relationship is to exchange money for merchandise. If the cashier throws your change back at you, or speaks to you in a nasty tone of voice, the respect dimension is compromised. This cannot be a healthy exchange and will affect your going to the particular register again, or even prevent you from shopping in that supermarket again. The unhealthy "cashier-customer" relationship alters your future behavior. On the other hand, if you have ever been to any of the Disney properties, your interaction with the "actors" is always expressed with care, honesty, and a tremendous amount of respect. You are greeted in a way that makes you feel important and comfortable.

Communication

A relationship with honesty, love/care, and respect creates a great deal of trust within that relationship. When all three are going strong, it is easy to put your faith, feelings, time, and even your body into that relationship without trepidation or question. You can depend on a person you trust. Trust is the outcome of a healthy relationship but the glue of the relationship is communication. The quality of the communication of honesty, love/care, and respect will be the determining factor in experiencing the presence of all three dimensions. Even if all three components are present, if they are not expressed they will not be felt in the relationship. Communication glues the relationship because it brings the presence of honesty, love/care, and respect to the other person's awareness. They do not have to wonder if they are present, they know it and can count on it. That is why the trust comes so easily in relationships that all three components are clearly communicated.

Communication takes two forms-verbal and nonverbal. Verbal communication is the spoken words used to express thoughts, feelings, opinions, criticism, and experiences. But words are not the only message sent when two people are communicating. Nonverbal messages are also transmitted. Nonverbal messages are body language, facial expression, tone of voice, and volume. Some linguists and psychologists believe that more than 60% of the true message a person sends to another person is sent in the nonverbal message as opposed to the actual words being spoken. It is easy to see how nonverbal messages can change the actual message. For example, if I said, *"Yes, Sharon, you are the sweetest person I know,"* you would probably say, *"Thank you, that was very kind of you."* But if I said the same exact sentence to you while rolling my eyes and smirking, you would probably not take too kindly to my message. My nonverbal message is contradicting the actual words spoken, and it is the nonverbal message you would react to, not the verbal message. Almost daily in my office I turn to a yelling husband or a wife, or a teenager and say, *"He can't hear you because you are talking too loudly."* It sounds like a ridiculous, illogical statement to say that someone can't hear because they are talking in too loud of a voice. I go on to explain that when you yell, the other person will only be responding to your anger, not your actual words. The volume of the message communicates anger and that will be the prevailing message. So, if you really want your words to be heard, lower the volume.

CHAPTER 6
Selfishless

*Give To Yourself*Give To Others*Give To The Group*

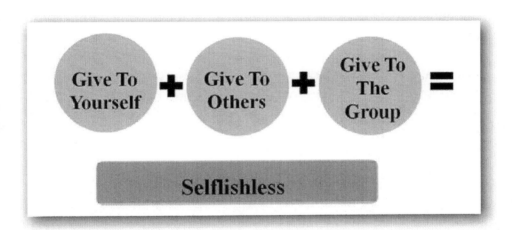

Give To Yourself

There are lots of cliché's about giving to yourself. Here are a few:

- If you don't love yourself, how can anyone else love you?
- Charity begins at home.
- Give back to others by giving to yourself first.
- The best gift you can give is to give to yourself.

As corny as cliché's usually are, they all have a semblance of truth to them.

Giving to yourself means that you need to spend a certain amount of time, energy, and money on yourself in order to meet your own physical needs, emotional needs, need for time, and need for specific material items. Giving to yourself is tantamount to self-respect. However, giving to yourself often feels and sounds like you are being selfish. The difference between being considered selfish and giving to yourself is a matter of degree. It is determined by how much and often you attend to your own needs as opposed to attending to other's needs.

I went to one of my high school reunions and spent a half hour talking to a fellow graduate. He wasn't even someone that was in my group of friends in high school but that doesn't seem to matter at high school reunions-you just talk to anyone. The cool and "in" crowd doesn't exist anymore (hopefully). Well, Tommy spent the entire half hour talking about how he took over his father's (already) successful business, providing me with the intricate details of how potato chips were made and shipped to supermarkets all over the northeast. I learned a lot about potato chips, it's packaging, and the details about how it is shipped so that it stays fresh. I learned a lot about Tommy, his bank account, and his family. Tommy, on the other hand, learned absolutely nothing about me, my family, or my life's accomplishments in the past 20 years. He never asked about me nor did he give me the opportunity to toot my own horn, as is almost protocol at high school reunions. My term, selflislessness, refers to a healthy balance between giving and taking in your relationships and in your life. My fellow high school alumni is an example of unbalanced selfishlessness.

Shelly

Shelly, a 42-year-old woman, entered therapy due to mild depression. During the course of her treatment she began discussing her relationship with her husband to whom she had been married for almost 20 years. It became increasingly more obvious to Shelly that she was extremely unhappy and no longer in love with her husband. She described him as a generally nice person, not abusive or even mistreating her in their relationship. It was merely a lack luster, loveless marriage. Shelly poignantly characterized her marriage as more of a roommate relationship than a romance. She began to flirt with the idea of divorcing her husband but was very indecisive. She wasn't afraid of being on her own, as she was a highly independent woman. She was somewhat concerned about what her financial situation would look like if they divorced but she believed she could make it work. The primary issue was her children. Shelly had 3 children, ages 15, 12, and 7 and she was afraid how a divorce would affect them. After all, they weren't living in a home that was fraught with hostility, anger, and arguments. A divorce would be a shock to them and the children had good relationships with both parents. Shelly grappled with the fact that she felt extremely guilty and selfish, pursuing her own happiness at the potential expense of her children.

Unfortunately, when you give to yourself it is sometimes at the expense of others-and often at the expense of the people you love most. To divorce or not to divorce-her thoughts bounced back and forth in her head like a ping-pong match. Shelly could have been Sharon, or Glenn, or Lisa-all patients of mine that are grappling with the same dilemma. All questioning whether or not they are being selfish if they divorce their spouses. At the same time, don't these patients all deserve to be happy in their lives? Are they being selfish or are they pursuing happiness by giving to themselves?

The opportunity to give to yourself isn't always as life altering as seeking a divorce to be happy in your life. There are countless situations that call for a decision between denying yourself something you want vs. giving to yourself. Sometimes they are daily occurrences such as taking that last piece of pie, or saying "no" to a friend who wants to borrow money when you are struggling in a responsible manner to manage your own finances, or choosing the restaurant you would like to go to even though your husband and children all want different restaurants to go to, or telling your friends that you are too tired to go out that Friday night because you had a stressful week at work.

Giving to yourself with both major and minor decisions can feel very good, if you can avoid feeling guilty about it. You deserve to be happy just as much as the people in your life that you give to on a daily basis. It can certainly be difficult negotiating whether or not to take something for yourself. You will need to take into consideration if meeting your needs affects others and how, and you need to consider how frequently you are giving to yourself instead of giving to others. Striking a balance between meeting your own needs and meeting the needs of others would be the ideal.

Giving To Others

It is as important to give to others as it is to make sure your needs are met. Again, the ideal is a balance between giving to yourself and giving to others in order to obtain a homeostatic state I refer to as "selfishlessness." Contrary to giving to yourself, giving to others will sometimes compromise your own needs or require giving up your time to benefit others. But, as I told a very sweet 9-year-old patient, every time you give to others it makes your heart grow bigger with love. Josh really took that to "heart." At his weekly appointments with me he began to report how much bigger his heart was because he gave to his Hebrew School donation fund, found a $5.00 bill and donated it to a local charity, and raked the leaves at his house to earn money for the soup kitchen. Giving to others builds your own character and feeds your self-worth and a feeling of meaningful, positive impact on others.

Giving to others takes on several different forms. Sometimes it is an act of kindness given to a stranger. Holding the door for someone, giving someone the right of way on the road, or giving a waitress an extra-large tip are examples of small but kind gestures. Donating your time and money to less fortunate people is another obvious way to give to others.

There is another form of giving to others that occurs within your everyday relationships. Whether it is a friend, colleague, family member, or spouse, there must be a certain amount of giving of yourself on a regular basis. Attending to their needs, problems, and making their life just a little bit easier goes a long way in solidifying your relationships. Offering them a ride, bringing them coffee, buying them lunch, and helping them solve a problem are all simple forms of giving in your relationships. Whether you are doing the little things for people or performing magnanimous gestures in your relationships or charity, giving to others goes a long, long way in cultivating and enhancing all of your relationships-including the relationship with yourself. You will be viewed by yourself and others as a generous person.

Giving Too Much To Others

The concept of balance has been mentioned several times with regard to walking the line between being selfish and selfless. Overly attending to your own needs at the expense of others will prevent you from having happy healthy relationships with others. It might make you happy in the short run because you will be getting almost all of your needs met, but it will drive people away from you because they are left high and dry in getting their needs met in the relationship. On the contrary, giving too much to others creates other kinds of problems in your relationships. Aliza, a 52-year-old wife and mother is a perfect example of what transpires when the needs of others are consistently placed in front of your own, almost always ignoring your own.

Aliza

Aliza is a homemaker, happily married, with two children. She entered therapy because she was worried that she was becoming depressed, and was confused by her feelings because she had a seemingly perfect life. She felt somewhat guilty for having her sadness, but there was a persistent sense of something missing or unfulfilled. At first she thought it was menopause but that explanation just didn't put her mind and her feelings at ease.

As sessions progressed I began to see a pattern in all of Aliza's relationships. She was always doing for others. She was the ultimate care-giver in all of her relationships including her mother, her 2 sisters, her husband, 2 children, and her friends. Early on in her treatment, she cancelled a session just a few hours prior to the scheduled time. When she eventually returned I inquired about why she had cancelled. As it turned out, her friend needed a ride to the car dealership because she needed to pick up her car which was being serviced. Her friend needed the ride at that time because she needed her car back in order to attend her exercise class, and then a dental appointment later in the afternoon.

I used this cancellation to highlight how Aliza seemed to put other people's needs in front of her own. She was denying herself her therapy appointment to accommodate her friend. On the surface it looks great. Everyone in Aliza's life knew they could count on her, no matter what. That made her a great friend. Or did it? What are her friends' reactions when dependable Aliza is physically unable to help them out? And what happens to Aliza's needs if she is constantly putting them aside or completely ignoring them? The result can be a feeling of depression and a sense of dissatisfaction.

Initially, Aliza was somewhat defensive. At first she minimized and rationalized it by saying, "What is the big deal? [Her] friend needed a ride and she would be charged for her exercise class even if she did not attend because of same day cancellation." Well, guess what Aliza, therapists also charge for late cancellations. That policy is not a business policy but rather it is a therapeutic issue. Patients need to maintain their motivation and commitment to the therapeutic process for it to be most effective. By putting her friend's transportation need in front of attending to her own needs, Aliza was diminishing her *own* importance.

Aliza began to recognize that giving to others and never saying, "no," was her way of coping with her own insecurity. Somehow, she equated denying requests made of her with rejection. In this situation, she realized that her friend had other friends, a sister living nearby, Uber, a taxi, the dealership, and even her son's car that he drove to school that day were possible alternatives if Aliza told her that she was unavailable to help her out.

As we explored her selflessness issue, she discovered that it was clearly at the route of her depressed feelings. There was very little left for Aliza by giving so much to others. It left her with an empty feeling and a feeling as if something was missing in her life. She also began to feel like a martyr and starting resenting the people in her life for taking advantage of her.

But that is not where the difficulty ended for Aliza. As she began talking about it with her husband and closest friend, and she learned that her selflessness also affected them in a negative way. They never really knew what she wanted when they asked her preference for social plans. Since she was so over accommodating, it was almost as if they didn't trust that she was expressing her true opinion on matters, or that she was merely saying what she thought they wanted to hear. That leads to frustration, mistrust, and feeling annoyed toward her. Clearly, Aliza needed to begin to give to herself and create more of a balance in her life. She needed to become less selfless.

Give To The Group

In addition to giving to yourself and giving to the people with whom you have relationships, there is a third aspect to giving. Giving to groups is another objective in your life that deserves your attention, time, consideration, and sometimes even money. Basically, there are three categories of groups you encounter throughout your life. The first type is the group that you do not actually participate in or are an official member of. Examples of this kind of group are typically charitable organizations, Red Cross, soup kitchens, and cancer research facilities. The second type of group is the group in which you are a member but you do not have a significant impact on the functioning of the group. Examples of this type of group are a religious affiliation with your church, temple, etc., the PTA, and the community in which you live. The third type of group is the type of group that you are an intimate member of and have a significant influence on the group's functioning and goals. Examples of this kind of group are family, work, extended family, friend groups, town council, or board member of a charitable organization. The third part of the Giving triad, Giving To The Group, has to do with the type of group that you have an active role in and help determine the group's functioning.

Group Roles

To better understand your impact on groups you need to understand the roles you play in the different groups in which you are a member. Each group has a distinct dynamic, or chemistry, and each group has a specific goal that gives the group purpose and identity. Sometimes the goal is a stated objective, and other times it is implied or subliminal. For example, your work group has a stated objective and is specifically evaluated in terms of that goal. But a family group has a subtler, less defined objective. The goals of your family group have to do with caring for one another, trust, and creating a sense of belonging and protection in order to sustain the group. The part you play in altering or contributing to the group goals may vary depending on the actual group. Your group role may also change from situation to situation within that group. To simplify possible group roles, I have narrowed them down to four possible roles you can play in the group. As you acquire an understanding of each group role, try to place yourself in the various groups to which you belong, and identify the roles you play in them.

The Mover
The first group role is called the "Mover." The Mover in a group does just like the name sounds. The Mover is the group member who gets the group to do things, to move towards its group goal, or to get the group to change. The Mover makes suggestions, institutes action, and often takes control of the group. Movers typically acquire power in a group, usually in a positive way. In your "friends" group, who is the one that initiates getting together for dinner? Who decides or suggests the restaurant or the time of the reservation? Do you ever play a mover in any of the groups to which you belong? Which groups and situations do you tend to play the Mover role? Know your role so you understand the impact you have on your groups and how you are influencing them. Evaluate which groups you are not playing the Mover and determine if your role should change to benefit the group's functioning or goals. That is part of giving to the group.

It can sometimes appear that group decisions are arrived at using a democratic process, but it is often driven by a Mover. The following is an example of a periodic interaction my wife and I will have on a Friday night. We will often go out to dinner on Friday nights. I will come home from the office after a week of seeing patients, giving presentations, and consulting with various organizations, and the following conversation periodically occurs.

I ask, *"Where would you like to go to dinner tonight?"*
"I really don't care; why don't you just pick a restaurant?" she responds.
"How about Firma's?" I suggest.
"Nah, I don't feel like Italian food tonight."
"How about the diner?"
"We went there last week."
I offer another suggestion. *"Thai Amin?"*
"Maybe."

Here's a good one, I think. *"We haven't been to Rachel's Grille in a while."*

She thinks, pauses, and says, *"That's a possibility. What about Thai Amin?"*

Since I *really* don't care, and having made 4000 decisions all week regarding patient care, I finally ask,

"Where would you prefer, Thai Amin or Rachel's Grille?"
"Let's go to Rachel's."
"Sure."

At the beginning of this conversation I am the Mover as I initiate the idea of going out for dinner. Then, my wife appears to relinquish her preference by seemingly allowing me to choose the restaurant. It appears as if we are making the decision together but in reality, she is the Mover, as she subtly is the one who ultimately chooses the restaurant. Since the decision really did not matter to me in the least, I acquiesce to the Mover. In other situations, depending on the activity, I am clearly the Mover. Your group role can change from group to group and situation to situation.

Movers are often group leaders but they do not necessarily have to be the ascribed leader. In other words, some groups, such as family groups, have ascribed leaders called the "parents." However, in many family groups the Mover turns out to be one of the children. The Sandstone family is a great example of how the mover of the family group is one of the children instead of the parents.

The Sandstone Family

Benjamin is a 10-year-old who has difficulty regulating his emotions. He can go from 0 to 60 with either anger or crying in a split second if he does not get what he wants, or if things don't go his way. He has two sisters, ages 8 and 5. They are relatively well behaved and have easy going personalities. Benjamin's behavior has greatly influenced his parents' decision making. Over the years, they have anticipated his disruptive response when they deny his requests. So, in order to avoid temper outbursts, they have evolved their parenting judgments to say "yes" to Benjamin even though they want to say, "no." In this case, Benjamin has become the Mover of the family because he is the determining family group member who determines what the family does. He chooses what the family eats for dinner, the Saturday afternoon family outing activity, and what television shows the three children watch on Sunday mornings. In order to keep the peace Benjamin's parents have enabled him to become the Mover of the family.

The Opposer

The Opposer role in a group also does just like the name sounds. The Opposer is the contrarian who generally works against the group goals or is disruptive to the group functioning. The Opposer is usually a negative person and has a negative influence on the group; however, the Opposer can also be an important member of the group who initiates positive change. Opposers usually go against the Movers in groups, which either interferes with group goals or functioning, or forces a positive change in the group goals or functioning. Some of the greatest men and women in history were really Opposers to the status quo regarding prejudice, racism, and social re-form. And others, on a more global scale, such as leaders of terrorist groups are Opposers who have a negative influence on the world population goal of living in peace and harmony.

Closer to home, think about the groups in which you are a member. Which groups or situations are you playing the part of the Opposer? Is it a negative or positive influence on the group's goals or functioning? The following example highlights how the Opposer can be a negative influence on a work group.

Devon The Downer

Devon is part of a market research team working in a large pharmaceutical company. The group consists of a project manager and 4 market researchers, including Devon. Their task is to determine how new drugs being launched should be marketed to the medical community. At team meetings Devon constantly shoots down ideas and suggestions. He finds fault with many ideas. He will talk about the project manager to his colleagues, criticizing her personality, leadership style, and marketing decisions.

Devon is an Opposer and has a negative influence on not only the group task and functioning, but also on the cohesiveness and morale of the group. Consequently, he negatively affects the group's productivity. In this case, as in many cases, Devon The Downer, the Opposer, is interfering with the group's ability to accomplish their task, or, at the very least, makes it more difficult to do so. You remember that old adage, "One bad apple spoils the bunch."

The Follower

Followers are group members who simply go along with the flow of the group. They rarely express opinions, move the group to action, or oppose the Mover. Followers tend to be passive individuals, easy-going, and easily satisfied. Groups need Followers as much as they need Movers and Opposers. Followers serve the positive purpose of supporting the group, and facilitating group function and attaining group goals. Followers are good soldiers and good team players. However, if a group has too many followers, it might stifle the group, slow it down, or even prevents it from reaching its goals.

The Bystander

The fourth group role plays the part of the Bystander. Bystanders do not contribute to the group in any positive ways. If Followers tend to be passive, Bystanders can be considered stationary. The Bystander has only a peripheral involvement in the group and does nothing to either help the group grow, meet the group goals, or support the group in any way other than to merely be a member of the group. However, Bystanders can be viewed as having a negative impact on the group because they do nothing to assist even when they recognize the need for their involvement.

The schoolyard playground at recess time is a setting that often exemplifies examples of Bystanders. When two or three kids are teasing a classmate, any child standing around watching the bullying are part of the group, but since they do nothing they are considered Bystanders. By doing nothing they are inadvertently contributing to the negative interaction of the group. Innocent bystanders are hardly innocent and do impact groups albeit in a very passive way.

When A Bystander Becomes An Opposer

I am fortunate enough as a parent to have many, many proud moments regarding my three children. But one of the stand-out proud moments occurred when my older son was a freshman in high school.

Daniel was sitting at dinner, early in his freshman year of high school, and he looked obviously troubled. I asked him if everything was alright and he said he was scared to go to school the next day. I asked him why, and he told me that there were two seniors teasing this other kid at lunch every day. He said the youngster being teased was a special education student. Daniel described him as socially awkward, a behavioral presentation that was probably consistent with the Autistic Spectrum. After listening to it for a few weeks and doing nothing about it, Daniel's social and moral conscience finally engaged. Having had enough, that day, Daniel stood up and confronted one of the seniors after the 17-year-old made some snide comments. Daniel stood up, approached one of the bullies and said, "Why don't you just leave him alone? He can't defend himself or help the way he is." Fortunately, the bell rang and the lunch aide approached them and told them to get to class. Daniel, a lowly freshman, was worried that the senior would seek him out the next day and start a fight with him. My wife and I offered to contact his counselor but, he insisted on handling the situation himself. Well, my faith in kids was renewed when Daniel came home from school the next day. He did not see either of the seniors until lunch period. One of them approached Daniel but instead of punching or berating him, the senior told Daniel that he thought about what Daniel told him the day before, and that he was sorry for being so mean. As it turned out, the senior was really a good kid and he was just following the other senior. Daniel gave him a wake-up call by reminding him what kind of kid he really was.

Your Group Roles
Giving to the group is entangled with the various roles you play in the groups in which you're a member. Remember, you need to think of groups not always as formal as work groups, family groups, or friend groups. You often find yourself involved in ill established, loosely-defined, and temporary groups. The playground example illustrates one such group. Nevertheless, you do play a role in informal groups, just as you play a role in your more well- defined groups. You need to identify the roles you tend to take in all groups in which you participate. Then, ask yourself if you are comfortable with those roles. Which roles do you need to change? Which situations are you playing the Opposer when you should be playing the part of the Follower? Which groups do you belong to that need you to become more of a Mover?

Groups usually need to keep growing. Your contribution, your giving to the group, involves maintaining or changing your group role so that the group both meets its goals, while the group continues to grow. Your family group is probably the most important group that needs your examination, evaluation, and potential changes in the group role you are playing. By examining your role and its effectiveness, you need to maintain a balance between contributing to the group needs and how the group meets your needs.

Compromising your needs too much in a specific group often results in resentment, anger, or even depression. Being too self-oriented in groups you participate in can lead to the group mistreating you, negative interactions with other group members or even rejection by the group. In evaluating your group roles, you need to not only identify whether your role is making a positive contribution to the group or not, but you also need to assess the balance between giving and getting from the group.

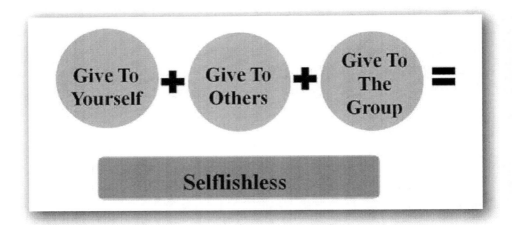

Selfishless

So, I created a new word. *Selfishless*. So that the train doesn't leave without you, you need to be selfishless. You need to be selfishless in order to seek happiness, freedom, and self-fulfillment in your life. Selfishlessness is an interpersonal skill that combines the act of being selfish with the act of being selfless. In other words, there are times when you need to be selfish and attend to your own needs, and times to give to others, even when it compromises your own needs. Being selfishless is creating a balance between the two.

You have an inner world and you have an outer world. Both worlds generate demands that need to be met. Your inner world consists of meeting your own needs and your outer world is comprised of all of the social, physical, and vocational demands that others place on you. The trick is creating a balance so that you are neither considered selfish nor selfless. Being selfishless is the ability to create that balance so that you are not considered to be selfish nor selfless.

By constantly self-monitoring how much you are taking care of your own needs, giving to others, and giving to groups, you can strike that healthy balance to create a state of selfishlessness. As is a good idea in all of the triads contained in this book, when you identify one of the three dimensions that is weakening or absent in your life, work on strengthening it or re-establishing it. You probably will never maintain an equal balance of the three in your life because demands are ever changing. The trick is to be aware of when one dimension needs attending to so that the train does not leave without you.

CHAPTER 7

Identity: Who Are You?

Uniqueness*Sense of Security*Tolerance

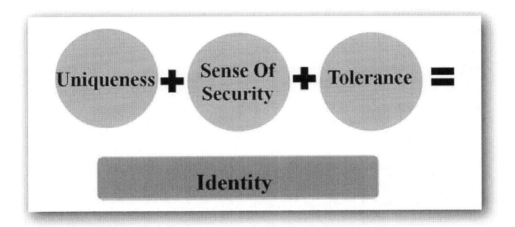

Uniqueness

The first task in being in touch with your identity is to recognize your uniqueness. Whether you see it or not, you have uniqueness about you. What are those factors that set you aside from everyone else on the planet? Sure, you have many similarities and can be outwardly identical to many people you know. Look hard and try to find distinctions in yourself. They are there. One of the things that have made me successful as a therapist is the fact that I can find that uniqueness in each and every patient. Uniqueness helps us feel special. Uniqueness helps us feel important and that we matter. Recognizing and accentuating your uniqueness helps define you as a person. It gives you character and definition. The people you come in contact with will find you to be an attractive person to be around. Identifying those traits or aspects of our personality, social relationships, and behavior patterns will help you make the train and not allow it to leave without you. Before you are able to identify those qualities that are distinctive, you must also identify those qualities that are common.

Recognize Your Commonness

A certain amount of commonness can be beneficial. Similar to almost all of the triads and concepts presented in this book, a balance between the two would be best. Commonalities between you and others help others relate to you and feel connected to you. It is not a coincidence that neighborhoods in cities become identified as the "Korean section, or the "Jewish neighborhood, or "Little Italy, because people with similar backgrounds, religious, and value systems congregate out of familiarity and comfort. Commonalities can be an interest or a hobby; it can be your value system; religious beliefs; moral attitudes and behavior; or specific personality traits such as easy-going or energetic. The things you have in common with others can be the initial attraction and can even sustain those relationships. But your unique qualities elevate the relationship to another level because if those commonalities are gone there is no basis left for the relationship to be sustained. An example of this phenomenon occurred for Maria, a young mother of a 3-year-old.

Maria immediately connected with Lisa when they began the Gymboree class with their daughters. They connected with toddler parenting issues, staying at home after working, and other similar life situations they shared. They eventually got together with the kids outside of the class. Then, the class ended. Maria kept initiating play dates with Lisa but to no avail. Lisa was always busy or found some vague excuse as to why she was unavailable. Maria's self-esteem was already somewhat fragile and she questioned why Lisa, who was always talking about her active social life, did not really want to be her friend. Maria finally realized that her friendship with Lisa was solely contingent upon the Gymboree class. She learned that Lisa was becoming close friends with another mother, Savannah, who was in their class. Savannah was a transplant from another part of the country and although she had many of the similar young mother of a toddler lifestyle commonalities, she also had a love for gardening. Lisa, growing up in a large city and now transplanted to the suburbs, always wanted to have a garden. Savannah's uniqueness set her apart from Maria, making her far more attractive as a friend. Lisa already had many friends that were similar to Maria.

Discovering Your Uniqueness

What is it about *you* that people would find interesting and different? Naturally, you aren't going to be the only one in the world with a specific quality, but you can certainly discover aspects of your identity that are not as common in your social circles or work environment. Finding your uniqueness requires an objective view of yourself. Many of your individual traits come so naturally to you that you simply take them for granted. How do you identify those parts of yourself that stand out? Do you perceive yourself as a competent person? Are you successful? We live in a highly competitive society where self-worth is most readily measured by our achievements. Self-esteem and self-worth tend to be highly contingent upon the accumulation of accomplishments-observable, measurable accomplishments. Getting a huge promotion, straight A's on a report card, scoring 3 goals in a game, and earning first place in a forensics competition are all signs of success and will certainly feed your self-worth and self-esteem. But we are often neglecting what I consider to be a lack of acknowledgement of some important personal attributes that exemplify your character and form your unique identity. These attributes are personality characteristics and deeds that are not necessarily awarded or rewarded with observable recognition. The fact is that we do not give awards for being sensitive to others, caring for others, giving of time, paying close attention to others' needs, good sportsmanship, and putting forth maximum effort even if the outcome is not the best.

Self-esteem and formation of identity are partially built by receiving the "best actress" Academy Award, the Most Valuable Player in Major League Baseball, Valedictorian of the class, or even getting the game ball for the winning hit, or a medal for first place in a 100-meter freestyle swim meet. These are public acknowledgements that validate competence and self-worth.

But what if you do not excel athletically, academically, or in the creative arts? This can result in having a low opinion of yourself, which is actually quite common. Since what we think and believe about ourselves is the basis for how we *feel* about ourselves, my therapeutic approach is to challenge my patients' belief system. Sometimes they have misbeliefs or irrational beliefs about themselves. Other times, people with low self-esteem actually have wonderful and valuable strengths that are simply not publicly revered. Consequently, these personal characteristics are not identified and do not register into a positive personal schema.

In therapy, there are non-specific aspects in the relationship between the therapist and patient that include perceived interest, attention, and caring by the therapist. When present, these attributes have been found to be as important in determining a positive therapeutic outcome as the actual therapeutic technique used by the therapist. It occurs in the sports arena as well. In basketball, assists are as important as baskets, in baseball, moving the runner over is as important as hitting him in, in football, it is making a great block allowing the running back to score. The work environment is no different. An employee that pays attention to details to avoid big mistakes and save the company money is as essential as the salesman who makes the huge sale. The receptionist in a law firm that treats each client as special and important does not directly account for the billable hours, but does make an important contribution to the overall experience of the client. The manager who keeps employees happy so that they remain invested, loyal, and productive is as important as the money that group makes for the company. These are all examples of how your uniqueness can serve you well and receive the recognition and personal satisfaction you deserve.

Take a look at yourself and others in your life and acknowledge important, unique traits that really make a difference and impact others in a positive way. Look at effort instead of outcome, the way others are treated instead of how attractive they are, give the game ball to sportsmanship, and the award for "The Most Benevolent." Taking these traits for granted does not enhance self-esteem and promote a sense of identity. Acknowledging them places value on them so that you and others can realize how you positively impact others in a special way that lasts a lot longer than receiving the award for "Best Salesman of the Year." Recognizing your special traits gives you a unique identity.

Sense of Security

Have you ever met someone who just seems to have an air of self-confidence? Not a braggart or arrogant person, but someone who just seems to have it all together. They know who they are and they know who they aren't. They are just okay with their strengths and weaknesses, accepting them in stride. They do not embellish their accomplishments nor do they become overly upset with their failures. Individuals with a good sense of security do not get flustered or defensive when someone confronts them. They simply handle life in a matter-of-fact, balanced manner.

When you have a sense of security within yourself, it provides you with a freedom from much angst and anxiety in your life. Self-doubt, feeling upset, and the whole gamut of emotions certainly are experienced, but usually in a productive, functional manner instead of a destructive, problematic manner. People with a positive sense of security are usually well-grounded, well-liked, and successful in their career and relationships. People with a positive sense of security know themselves well, and are comfortable with their identity. There are many powerful benefits to having a good sense of security.

Accept New Challenges

When you have a sense of security you are more willing to accept new challenges in life. A common reaction when faced with something different or challenging in life is to become anxious. That anxiety comes from an automatic belief that you might fail or not accomplish that challenge. An insecure person fears failure and may try to avoid that terrible feeling of failure. Someone who has a sense of security will accept that challenge because their sense of self and competence does not hang on a thread. The challenge is not threatened by the prospect of failure so there is no fear or anxiety. They maintain their motivation because they accept the belief that it is okay to fail. That it doesn't mean I am worthless or inept. When the fear of failure is diminished, new challenges are embraced. Sometimes you may not be successful, but other times you will succeed. The mere fact that you are trying and not avoiding new people or tasks in your life promotes positive change in you and your identity.

Expanding your horizons leads to happiness, freedom, and self-fulfillment. A willingness to try new things prevents the train from leaving without you.

Receptive To Criticism

Being corrected, told you are doing something wrong, or being criticized are part of life. You will make mistakes and people will notice. I often tell patients that we can't make it a goal that you will never make a mistake. A more realistic goal is to try to only make a mistake one time and never repeat it.

Having a strong sense of security helps you deal with criticism and correction in a productive way instead of a potentially destructive way. When you are sure of yourself and can readily accept weaknesses and mistakes, you will use feedback from others as a way to either reinforce your convictions or make positive changes in your life. As you and your identity continue to evolve throughout your life, modifications and major changes may need to occur. Many changes are often precipitated by someone, who has a significant impact on you, providing you with criticism or correction. Having a sense of security allows you to look at that external feedback and evaluate its validity in a more objective manner. If you are insecure, there will be many cognitive and emotional filters that will skew the criticism to the point that you can easily invalidate it. In one of Woody Allen's movies he said something like, "Sometimes you are not paranoid, it's that people are really after you." Well, sometimes when people criticize you it is actually accurate and useful. If you, due to your insecurity filters, alter the criticism then you will undoubtedly discard it to preserve your already fragile self-esteem. Having a good sense of security enables accurate and objective interpretation of criticism leading to your growth as a person. Growth and self- improvement are very much a factor in living a happy, free, and self-fulfilling life.

Positive Relationships

I was recently on the beach in Mexico and there was a tee-shirt vender making his rounds among the tourists. He was wearing one of his wares, promoting his product. It said, *"Who needs Google, my wife knows everything."* Of course, it's funny, but the guy who wrote that is expressing annoyance with his wife through sarcasm. Perhaps she criticizes him too much or never helps him feel that his way is the better way. That would be her insecurity. If he has a positive sense of security, he will not take issue with her always being "right" and handle it in a positive way. He will not allow feelings of anger or annoyance to interfere in his relationship with her because he can objectively see when she is right about something, and when he needs to gently reject her ideas.

Interactions in relationships, both positive and confrontational situations, will go better if you have a sense of security. It promotes a positive relationship. My in-laws exemplified a great example of how a sense of security prevents strife in a relationship. My father-in-law would announce that he is taking out the trash and the conversation would go something like this.

He would announce, *"I'm going to take out the trash."*
My mother-in-law would then yell to him from another room, *"Paul, put a coat on its cold outside."*
He would respond, *"I'm not cold and I'm just going outside for a minute."*
"Put a coat on anyway," she would say.

He would then put a coat on and turn to me and say, *"We're one person-HER!"*

But he wouldn't get angry and he wouldn't argue with her. He would just do it for the sake of the relationship and choose more important topics to argue about. It takes a sense of security to be able to do that. A sense of security helps you not be defensive and feel threatened in relationships. Defensiveness destroys relationships. Some people have an armor of defensiveness and are heavily defended. A sense of security also enables you to readily accept the positive affections and attention by others instead of rejecting them. If you feel insecure, your schema may be a negative one. So, when positive feedback comes your way you might reject it because it is incongruent with your image of yourself. You might believe that it is unfounded or false. This is evident when you compliment someone and they either dismiss it, give someone else the credit, or minimize their accomplishment.

Better Coping

Since mistakes and failures are a part of everyone's life, we need to learn how to effectively cope with our unsuccessful endeavors. Coping skills begin developing in early childhood. Some are helpful and adaptive and others are harmful and maladaptive. Having a good sense of security enables us to develop positive coping mechanisms and strategies instead of destructive ones.

The patient that told me he was failing his Monday morning class blamed it on the train leaving without him. This, rather ineffective way to deal with his failure, displaces blame on others. You will not change a maladaptive behavior, in this case, making the train on time, unless you take responsibility and ownership for the problem. Having a good sense of security allows you to look at yourself and determine what your part of the failure or mistake you are causing. Once you are able to identify your ownership in the problem, you can then problem solve to make effective changes.

It would be prudent to try to identify the coping and defense mechanisms you have developed at this point in your life. Do you displace blame, make excuses, rationalize, justify, minimize, or completely deny when you are confronted by others? None of these coping strategies will lead toward positive changes in your life and in your relationships. Making it okay to make mistakes and experience failure by coping effectively means you have a good sense of security. It also means that you will most likely preempt major battles due to escalation of conflict and anger by you and others in your life.

Maintain Perspective

Perspective will be addressed in more detail in Chapter 12. For now, understand that having a good sense of security helps you maintain perspective. It allows you to maintain objectivity about yourself, your world, and your interactions with others. Maintaining perspective tempers your reactions and prevents over-reactions. It also prevents under-reactions. Just going through life helps you gain perspective. Having a psychological practice for almost forty years now, I believe I have a wonderful perspective in determining how dysfunctional or serious a patient's issues or illness is. Having prior experiences and learning from them is the first step in having perspective. Learning how to apply them to the present situation is the key step.

That sense of security that you are working toward gives you the perspective and knowledge to effectively deal with most situations. This especially applies to someone with whom you have had a long term relationship. If you know how they tend to react to certain situations, you can gauge your reaction with good perspective. Matthew, a 54-year-old patient provides us with an example of how gaining perspective improved two issues he was having with his wife.

Matthew Gains Perspective

Matthew has been married for twenty-four years. He and his wife love to entertain. The first few years of their marriage he noticed that his wife became extremely up-tight when preparing dinner for guests. She would become short-tempered and unreasonable. She would ask him to do unnecessary tasks such as dust on top of the entertainment center, go to the store to get more carrots when they had 4 times the amount they already needed, or vacuum the living room rug-for the third time. At the beginning of their marriage Matthew would argue with her and try to reason with her about these unnecessary tasks. That would only inflame her. It took some time, but he eventually realized, with perspective, that this was her anxiety about having everything "just right" for their guests. That it had nothing to do with him or her trying to be overly controlling, which is what he initially thought. So, he simply stopped arguing and challenging her. He started doing everything she asked, even if she wanted the kitchen floor licked clean. He first noticed that she started asking him to do things and as he began to do them she would change her mind and say, "never mind." After a longer period of time, Matthew noticed that her irrational requests completely stopped. That wasn't because of the change in his reaction. His wife became more secure with her entertaining. That evolved from her own perspective through many successful dinners. Matthew's perspective regarding her pre-entertaining behavior prevented it from escalating into a power struggle and huge arguments in their relationship. In effect, having bitter feelings toward one another would probably have tainted their ability to help their guests feel comfortable and successfully entertain them.

Tolerance

The third piece of the identity triad is tolerance. You must have a certain amount of tolerance for yourself and tolerance for others. The specific tolerance referred to here is tolerance for differences in you and tolerance in differences from people in your life, as well as for any person you encounter in the world. Tolerance encompasses many aspects and they all require a lack of, or minimal emotional response. That is, when you encounter someone that is very different from you, or if there is something different about someone with whom you have a social relationship, you accept it without feeling threatened by it, trying to change it, or reacting in a negative emotional manner to that difference. Instead of trying to impose *your* way of thinking, tolerance requires you to be nonjudgmental and involves a great deal of acceptance of individual differences. Tolerance for others means not judging them based on your values. Respecting their individual identities is the same as tolerating their differences even when they are alien to your way of thinking or living. Always remember that "different" is not necessarily "bad," it is just different.

Tolerance in yourself is equally as important as having tolerance in others. You must be able to tolerate the fact that you have weaknesses or flaws. Part of your identity is how you define yourself, and part of it is your strengths and weaknesses. It is the weaknesses that will require you to maintain tolerance so that they don't create low self-esteem or inappropriate emotional reactions.

Open-Mindedness

Being open-minded is a big part of having tolerance. If you are receptive to other ideas, values, behaviors, and moralities, you can not only improve your relationships with those who are different from you, you can modify your own identity. Often, by being open-minded, you encounter some intriguing and attractive new ways of thinking, and new experiences that add to your life in a positive way.

Stubbornness, or being rigidly set in your ways, does not allow for open-mindedness. Narrow thinking cuts you off from experiences and people that could enhance your life. At the very least, when you are open-minded and receptive you may reject many novel ideas but it puts you in a position to take advantage of something that may contribute positively to your life and the kind of person you are. Having enough tolerance for differences can add to your relationships and your identity.

Patience

Tolerance involves patience. So often in life's endeavors and in specific moments, time is the best intervention for resolution to problems. Giving another person, or a specific tumultuous situation time to resolve on its own requires a great deal of patience. For this to occur, you will need to patiently tolerate the anxiety or frustration experienced until the problem is resolved.

There is a direct relationship between the amount of patience required and the level of intimacy in the relationship. Patience is tested more often and more emotionally in romantic and family relationships. These are the people in your life that you feel most comfortable being yourself and saying what you think. With others, you will usually have a modicum of company manners. Closer, more intimate relationships require more patience because of the amount of time you spend together. Patience requires you to bite your tongue, even when it is apparent that the other person is in error. Tolerating their opinion or actions with your patience often allows them to make their own corrections without you having to criticize or correct them.

Resilience

Tolerance, in the realm of stamina and endurance, is synonymous with resilience. Resilient people are able to sustain their positive attitude during difficult times. Resilient people have stamina and strength to forge ahead even when they are repeatedly knocked down. A great deal of inner strength and fortitude are exhibited by resilient people. Their ability to endure adversity and bounce back repeatedly requires a great deal of tolerance. Tolerance of frustration, failure, and discouragement.

Resilience cannot be taught to you by another person. It can be modeled and you can emulate other resilient people. Think about the most resilient person in your life and use them as a model for how they would handle your specific or life situations. Their tolerance and resilience can guide you through difficult times and you can begin to incorporate resilience into your own identity.

Resilience is also a mind-set. Just like everything else in life, it is all how you think about it. You can train yourself, using self-talk, to tolerate the demands being placed on you and rise to the occasion. You can actually talk to yourself and put yourself in the frame of mind to keep trudging on, to sustain your efforts, and maintain your strength even in the face of great adversity. Do not allow others stuff affect you and your life, so tolerate it without getting involved or letting other people's stuff affect you, your feelings, or your life.

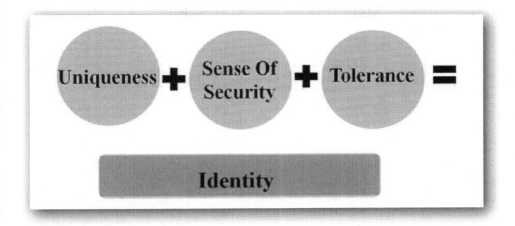

Identity

As is the case in other triads discussed thus far, there is a direct interrelationship between the 3 components; being unique, having a sense of security, and having tolerance. These 3 factors enable you to crystallize your individual identity so that you feel empowered and secure. Recognizing and emotionally accepting your uniqueness and tolerating your flaws places you in a position to feel secure with yourself. Tolerance for yourself and tolerance for others is tantamount to respecting your uniqueness and the differences between you and others. Having tolerance is also directly connected to your sense of security because the more secure you feel within yourself, the more tolerant you can be for differences in others. In other words, being secure prevents you from feeling emotionally threatened by another person being different from you. In a nutshell, if you know who you are, and you know who you aren't, and you are able to feel okay with whoever you are, your identity will be secure.

Cameron's Identity

Cameron, a 21-year-old Division 3 Lacrosse player came to see me after learning that his best friend, dorm and road-game roommate, Rob, revealed to him that he was gay. Initially, Cam did not react to his friend. They both kept it private, as Rob was not officially "out." Cam found himself becoming short-tempered with his friend, picking on little things like a dirty juice cup or dirty laundry left in the room. He became distant and started not acting "like himself" when he was around Rob.

In therapy, Cameron discovered that his gradually developing negative emotional reaction toward his friend was due to his lack of tolerance for Rob's sexual preference. He thought he was open-minded about homosexuality, adopting a "live and let live" attitude but this time it was close to home. He discovered that he himself was not all that comfortable with his sexuality that it made it difficult to tolerate the difference in Rob. Cam was not gay, but because of his questioning of his own sexuality his sexual identity confusion became heightened when exposed to diversity in others. It became an emotional threat to his sense of security, his own uniqueness, and his ability to tolerate differences in others. That all translated into his mistreating his best friend resulting in his feeling guilty and ashamed.

Cam quickly arrived at the source of his problem and was able to resolve it once he became comfortable with his own identity. He was then able to regain his close friendship with Rob because he was able to solidify his own sense of self so that his friend's sexuality was not an emotional threat to him.

Identity: Create It, Understand It, Accept It

Who are you? Do you know? Your identity, as you understand it and express it, is the foundation of your uniqueness, sense of security, and tolerance of differences in others. How you define yourself establishes the type of relationships you have, your occupation, and how you see yourself. Your identity is comprised of your qualities, a consistent set of personality traits, a consistent set of behaviors, and how you present yourself morally and ethically. Your identity is an identifier to yourself and others, consisting of personal preferences, mannerisms, values, personality traits, hobbies, and your own uniqueness or quirkiness.

We all have an internal identity, or schema. Your schema is your view of yourself. Sometimes, an individual's internal schema does not match their external identity. This is usually not done purposely and can create self-esteem and relationship problems. I once had a stunning (by all accounts) Madison Avenue model as a patient who had low self-esteem and felt ashamed and guilty that she was paid an exorbitant amount of money for photographers to take pictures of her. She did not see herself as pretty so her internal schemata did not match the world's message that she was beautiful.

How you see yourself is entangled with self-esteem, self-worth, and your sense of adequacy. These are quintessential factors in facilitating your happiness, freedom, and self-fulfillment. When your identity is secure it defines you. The problem is that your identity is not static. It is fluid, forever changing throughout the course of your life. Identity is ever changing but as you get older changes are usually limited to modifications, minor adjustments, and alterations.

Believe it or not, identity actually begins forming as an infant. As you began to interact with your environment, finding ways to get your needs met such as hunger, sleep, and a soiled diaper, you begin to define your sense of self in relation to your environment. Accidentally knocking into the mobile hanging over your crib and experiencing the motion of the object creates something called effectiveness motivation. That gratifying experience provokes your motivation to intentionally hit it with your hand. When you successfully accomplish this amazing feat, it is the beginning of your competence motivation. You actually had an effect on your environment and you begin to differentiate your body from your surroundings. This is the beginnings of identity because it is your first experience that effects change that provides you with inner pleasure.

As a developing child your identity has a foundation. During adolescence, identity formation accelerates. Adolescence is a developmental period when your identity is further crystallized and defined. It is a time of your life when you actually try on a variety of different "hats" with the developmental task of setting the stage for your young adult and later adult life. Post high school training, college major, and career path are a large part of the late adolescent and early adulthood identity.

As stated earlier, identity is relatively fluid, changing in accordance with your particular developmental period in life. But, sometimes it is an external event or changing life situation that initiates a more dramatic identity change.

Examples of such external events are the death of a parent or life partner, divorce, or being terminated from your job of 15 years. Sometimes, it is a shift in family situation as Jacqueline, a 47-year-old mother of 4 children, ages 16 to 22 discovered.

From Homemaker To Entrepreneur

Jacqueline is a dedicated mother, living in an upper middle class town. Her husband is extremely successful and finances have never been an issue. Their family subscribed to traditional gender roles whereas Philip worked outside the home to provide financial resources for the family and Jacqueline managed the home and children. She car-pooled, made lunches, went to school events, cooked, cleaned, and chauffeured the kids to doctor's appointments, SAT tutoring, sporting events, and friends' houses. With the children reaching an age where they are relatively self-sufficient, even driving themselves, Jacqueline found her role in the family diminishing. Her children simply did not need her as much anymore. Two were even away at college most of the year now.

Jacqueline started her own business. She bought a local store selling home furnishings in the way of knick-knacks and small decorating items for the home. She had an art and design background from her art major in college and her career prior to having children. Jacqueline had essentially put her creative identity on hold for the duration of her marriage with children.

Interestingly, as she became increasingly more involved and successful in her business, her marriage began to experience significant conflict. Philip, who used money as power and control in their relationship, began to feel threatened. With Jacqueline's identity change, she became more independent from her husband, was not as available to him, and began to raise her status in the relationship. Philip had difficulty adjusting to his wife's new "identity."

When your identity shifts noticeably, it affects others in your life. This causes them to interact with you differently. As you make changes in your life, you need to keep this ripple effect in mind.

PART TWO
The Nitty Gritty

CHAPTER 8

Work Ethic

*Play Vs. Work*Organizational Skills*Excellence*

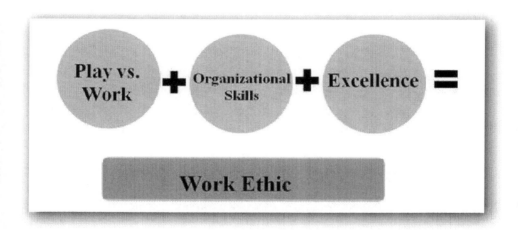

Play Vs. Work

Work ethic, specifically work vs. play issues, was briefly touched upon in Chapter 3. Distinguishing between work time and play time is the cornerstone of having a good work ethic. We are not born being able to discriminate between the two. It is something we learn, hopefully, as we develop. In fact, the beginnings of a sense of industry, the need to achieve and accomplish, is actually developed at a very young age. It usually begins during the first formal educational experience. That can be in a pre-school program, or in Kindergarten.

Initial formal educational experiences begin to place demands on children to complete a task. The task is expected to be started, worked on, and completed within the time frame specified by the classroom teacher. When you think about it, most of the school day is structured in this same manner. It is the teacher directing and expecting tasks to be completed on his or her time schedule. Work is thrust upon kids despite the fact that they probably would rather play. It is easy to understand how the rudiments of work vs. play starts with formal schooling. As we progress through the school grades, coupled with our parents placing "work" demands on us, we develop the distinction between work time vs. play time.

So, if that is how work vs. play develops through educational experiences and parental demands, why do so many of us have difficulty disciplining ourselves? Why do we often find ourselves in crisis trying to get things done at the last minute; or forgetting to do things; or failing to meet deadlines; or even purposely refusing to complete work related tasks? The answers to these questions are very complicated with a multitude of possible reasons ranging from Attention Deficit Hyperactivity Disorder to the immature need to just play and shirk work. We can explore these reasons but that would cover an entirely different book. Suffice for our purpose; we can break it down to a painfully simplistic explanation.

Work Is Work And Play Is Fun

Let's face it, even those who love their work would rather play because work is work and play is fun. Despite teachers and parents' attempt to teach us to attend to our work in lieu of play, we, as adults, often do not do so. What invariably happens as we grow and develop is that we begin having more freedom as to how we choose to spend our time. Think about it. A 5-year-old is closely supervised by his or her parents and how they spend their day is completely driven by parents. A 15-year-old has a lot more discretion as to how he or she spends their day. At 25-years-old the decision as to how their day is spent is completely within their own decision.

In the absence of a teacher or parent directing and demanding, the play part of work vs. play frequently wins over. At work, it is usually not a problem because it replicates your time as a child when some adult was telling you what to do and when to do it. Your boss is the "adult" you are answering to at work so you will have less difficulty discriminating between work and play time. But once it is solely up to you, when no one else is telling you to do the laundry now, or clean the kitchen, or pay your monthly bills, or go through that pile of papers sitting on the dining room table, you will be inclined to play instead.

Self-Discipline

The struggle between taking care of your tasks and engaging in pleasurable activities, has everything to do with your drive for need gratification. Our brain, more specifically, our neurological system has to develop the ability to either delay or deny our need for gratification. We have a need for something or an activity that provides us with pleasure. If we are lucky, we get to satisfy that need immediately. More often than not, we have to either wait or deny ourselves that pleasure either because the timing is inappropriate to get it, or it is unreachable or inappropriate for us to acquire that pleasure. This is where self-discipline and establishing limits enters into the equation to self- impose discipline between your work time and play time.

The ability to say "no" to yourself when you want to say "yes" is a necessary skill in developing a good work ethic. You must adopt a "work first and play later" philosophy in your life. Not allowing yourself to play before all your work is done will prevent both minor and major problems in your life. One way to help yourself delay your play is to set up reward contingencies surrounding your present work tasks. Establish specific work tasks or responsibilities that require your immediate attention and provide yourself with a "play" reward once these tasks are accomplished.

Don't Shirk Work Benefits

There is a great irony in this work vs. play paradigm. It was stated earlier that work is work and play is fun. The irony is that the more work you do, the better you handle your responsibilities both large and small in your life, the more play you end up getting. That means delaying and denying many pleasures in the moment and taking care of your responsibilities so that you can reap the benefits of pleasures at a later date. This applies to the immediate pleasures as well as the long run benefits.

When you take care of your daily tasks, it frees you up to enjoy your pleasures with a clear conscience and mind. That allows you to enjoy them to the fullest. If you are playing a video game, reading a great novel, or watching a television show instead of completing a task that needs immediate attention, your mind cannot be fully on the enjoyable activity because the task is lingering. The other thing that can happen is that by not attending to the immediate task, it may have an impact on your next day which prevents you from engaging in an even more desirable activity. Raymond, a 34-year-old, experienced this situation when he chose to play World of Warcraft (WOW), an online video game, for 4 hours one evening instead of organizing his financial records in preparation of meeting with his accountant. By putting it off a day, he had to decline an invitation for a free ticket to an NBA playoff ticket for his favorite team. The ticket was probably valued at $500 and the opportunity was priceless since his team rarely made the playoffs. If he went to the game that next night, he would not be able to meet with his accountant and complete his tax preparation. Why didn't he postpone his meeting with the accountant and go to the game? Because he kept postponing the meeting and now the deadline for filing his taxes was upon him. If he just took an hour or two to collect all his information instead of playing WOW, he would be going to the basketball game. By attending to your work first you end up with providing more options for yourself.

The more responsible you are by attending to your work demands, the more play opportunities you are afforded in the long run as well. Education is a prime example of long run benefits. If you take care of your training program or schoolwork and requirements, you end up getting an education that affords you with a career that pays you enough money to purchase things and go places that you choose. Without successfully completing a course of training your earnings potential may be limited precluding you from purchasing and doing things you really would want. The ideal situation occurs when your work and your play are the same thing. That occurs when you love your career or job to the point where you actually enjoy going to work. You need to work to support yourself and the work you are doing is something you like to do. When this happens, your work and play are the same. Taking care of work first and getting your play later helps you control your life and seize opportunities so that the train does not leave without you.

Organizational skills

In the English language, when a noun takes on the suffix *"ize"* it becomes a verb. For example, the noun *scrutiny* becomes *scrutinize*. The root word of scrutinize is scrutiny. The noun *fossil* becomes *fossilize*. To make *sterile* a verb it becomes *sterilize*. Do you think the word *organ* is made into a verb by making it *organized?* It would make perfect sense if it is derived from the root word organ because healthy human organs function efficiently, consistently, and flawlessly 24 hours a day. Just as body organs function, being organized means that you need to be efficient, consistent, and attempt to be flawless.

Leading an organized life is important because it helps you have a good work ethic. Being organized will streamline your life and help reduce undue stress and prevent last minute crises because of time constraints. Organization makes your life run smoothly which enables you to cope better with the occasional curve balls life throws at you. Sometimes the train leaves without you because the wrong departure time was listed. Sometimes, you are missing out on great things in life because you couldn't get your act together to make the train.

Organizational Strategies

When you are organized your life becomes somewhat more predictable. An organized life tends to be a more structured life. You do things in the same way, in the same order, and at the same time. Becoming organized means building in specific routines in your life. When I come into my office every morning, the first thing I do is put my car keys on a specific bookshelf. It is always the same bookshelf unit; always the same shelf; and always the same spot on that shelf. This routine is almost mindless at this point. I automatically place the keys on that shelf every morning. I don't even have to think about it. That simple, automatic routine helps me in two ways. First, at the end of the day, I don't have to spend any time looking for my keys. I know exactly where they are because I am organized enough to place them in the same spot. I know where to find them. It saves me time. The second benefit to this routine occurs when I need to bring something home from the office that it not part of my routine. For example, if I need to bring a file home or a flash drive I place a sticky note right next to my keys, or I place the flash drive right next to my keys. By associating novel tasks with routinized procedures I do not need to rely on my memory at the end of the day to bring these items home. All I do is automatically reach for my keys and BAM! the novel items are sitting right there to remind me.

Being organized also entails putting things in the same place all the time. Look around your home and make sure that everything has a place. As you use these items, always place them back in their spot, and do it immediately. Putting things off saves you a minute or less of time by not doing it right now. But, if you forget where you put it and need it again, you can spend several minutes or more looking for it. That is not to mention the stress and frustration that occurs until you find it.

When you organize your "things" you need to use logic. Place things in a logical place and in a logical order. In your kitchen, the coffee cups should be in the cabinet above the coffee machine. The most frequently used food category should be the most accessible with the rare food products up high or in the back of the cabinet. Your space at work should also be organized in a logical order and items placed strategically. Take a look at it one day when you have a clear head and rearrange your desk and work space so that it creates an ease of accessibility and efficiency. As you go through your work day and perform daily tasks, think about how your work materials can be moved for easier access. Sometimes moving the stapler or rearranging your desk drawer can save you time, effort, and aggravation. The same goes for organizing your computer desktop and files for quick access.

Organizing your technology is also a great strategy to maintain and organized life. If you aren't tech savvy, find someone who can rearrange your computer or tablet so that your most frequently used programs are easily accessible. Create shortcuts or have someone teach you how to use shortcuts. On your mobile phone, create speed dial contacts. Number them in a logical order so that it is easy to remember. I have my wife as speed dial number "1" and each of my 3 children on speed dial numbers "2" through "4" from the oldest to the youngest. It is logical, easy to access and easy to remember. Logic is a great tool for organization.

Organizing your "things" will certainly help you lead an organized life. But, that is not enough. You will need to organize your time, as well. Organizing your time is tantamount to managing your time. Time management is a life skill. Imagine if Charlie, my college student patient who kept missing the train could manage his time better. He would have been passing his Monday morning class and I would have to think of a different title for this book!

Managing Time

A large part of having a good work ethic lies in the ability to manage your time.
Managing your time means:

- being planful with your time
- being efficient with your time
- accurate judgment of the amount of time it takes to complete specific tasks
- treating your time and others' time with value and respect
- being prepared for surprises

Time is the most precious commodity in your life. To live a happy, free, and self- fulfilled life you need to maximize the use of your time and treat it as delicately and special as possible. Remember, you cannot recapture time once it is spent. Every minute, hour, or day that passes is lost without the ability to redo it. All that remains of time spent is the memory of what you did during that time period. Everyone has past regrets, but if you don't want the train to leave without you and have many and major regrets in your life, you will concentrate hard on managing your time well.

Being Planful

Maintaining a calendar of events is the most useful way to be planful with your time. The most practical calendar to maintain is an electronic calendar that is synced in "the cloud" to all of your devices including tablet, mobile phone, home computer, and work computer. Electronic calendars are a powerful tool and serve as an extra "brain" for you because you do not have to remember appointments. Electronic calendars such as iCloud and Google Calendars have features that structure your time and utilize features such as alerts, repeating events, appointment invitation for others, and appointment sharing with others.

Creating audible alerts for overly important or rarely occurring events makes it virtually impossible for you to forget to attend them. Audible alerts are especially useful for events occurring randomly, once a week, every quarter, or even yearly. Despite the usefulness of alert features, you need to check your calendar first thing every morning, last thing every night, and frequently during the day. This book is largely about taking and maintaining control over your own life. Contrary to this notion, your electronic calendar is something in your life that, in a way, runs your life. It tells you what to do, when to do it, and with whom. The fact that you are the one commanding the calendar by inputting the appointments means that you really are the commander of your life. The calendar just tells you what you have set up for yourself but you need to rely on it to tell you where you need to be and when you need to be there.

If you are digitally challenged, a paper calendar is the next best thing. The problem with a paper calendar is the impracticality and lack of 24/7 accessibility to it. You can maintain a work and home calendar but you will not be able to access it when you are not with that particular calendar. Almost everyone knows how to use the photo App on their mobile phone. One way around accessing home calendars at work and vice versa is to take a picture of each calendar at the end of each day.

Inserting events and appointments in your calendar requires thought and contemplation. Being planful is to make sure you build in an accurate duration for each event, travel time between events, and the physical and emotional drain of the event. You want to try to avoid scheduling a visit to your mother with third stage Alzheimer's in the assisted living facility and a meeting with your divorce attorney back to back or even in the same day. Structuring your day and week must take into consideration all of these factors to avoid over scheduling.

Maintaining a calendar for events and appointments is only one aspect of being planful with your time. You also have daily tasks that need to be completed. Once again, we turn toward our electronic devices to help us be more planful with completing daily tasks. Using the Reminder App on your mobile device and syncing it to the cloud will make your task list available on all of your devices identical to your calendar's syncing. No matter where you are, if you have any one of your devices with you, you can consult your Reminder App to tell you what needs to be done. Most Reminder Apps enable prioritizing and categorizing your tasks. As with your calendar, you can use alert features for specific task, placing the due date, a reminder prior to the due date, and deadline for its completion. Just as with your calendar, you need to check your reminders list frequently throughout the day so you do not forget to complete any task.

There is no limit to the detail or extent of the tasks to be listed in your Reminders App. Everything from buying a birthday card for your sister, to calling your accountant to file your taxes, to completing your quarterly sales report should be entered. Everything and anything that needs to be done can be placed in your categorized lists. You can also integrate both your calendar and reminders list by blocking time in your calendar to complete tasks on your reminders list.

Being Efficient

In addition to structuring your time and tasks you need to be efficient. As mentioned earlier, plan your meetings and events carefully. If you have the flexibility, plan back to back events that are in close proximity to each other to save driving time. Being efficient with your time is using time wisely. Try to avoid doubling your efforts. Some tasks are related to one another and can be completed more efficiently. Some tasks can be completed by piggy backing. For example, if you need to do your laundry, which involves waiting time for the washer and drying stages, look at your list and complete those tasks that coincide with washer and drying times. In effect, you will be completing several tasks at the same time.

Most electronic Calendar Apps allow you to color code your events. By color coding your social, work, medical, etc. events you can quickly scan your calendar to see what your day or week looks like without even reading the actual event. Color coding your appointments also gives the calendar a more pleasing and easier to the eye appearance to help you not feel overwhelmed.

You can also color code the categories in your Reminders App. Categories can be endless and tailored to your life needs. Some examples, but by no means limited to, are:

- Call Backs
- To Do
- Reminders
- Dinner Ideas
- Bills
- Books to Read

By color coding your category titles you can efficiently and easily select the tasks you need to take care of in the moment. All lists should be examined regularly so as not to forget about completing any of them.

Judging Time

Part of using your time well is being able to judge the time it takes to accomplish tasks. So often people misjudge the amount of time it takes to complete a task and it is usually an underestimate. Thinking that it only takes 15 minutes to clean out your garage when it really takes 2 hours can really put a kink into your schedule for that day.

Judging time accurately entails really putting some thought into the task. You should first break down the task step by step in your mind to have a more realistic view of what the task entails. Another way to accurately judge the time it takes to complete a task is to recall how much time it took to complete it if you have done it previously.

By not judging time well you tend to create more stress in your life because you will often be behind schedule. Certain tasks will not be done or will be done at a later date because you run out of time. Remember, time is finite. There is only so much of it available to you so you will need to use it wisely.

Value And Respect Time

Valuing and respecting your time is more of an attitude than a specific strategy to manage your time. The suggestion here is to maintain a certain attitude toward your time that sustains the idea that your time is limited and precious. Giving your time reverence preserves its importance and value. Treating it as a precious commodity in your life will help keep you in a mindset to be more planful, more efficient, and judge your time in a productive manner.

Prepare For Surprises

There is an adage that states, "We plan and God laughs." The root of this message is that life will often throw surprises or unexpected events your way. Even the best laid plans accounting for all possible variables can be interrupted by unexpected situations or factors. Managing your time well and having a good work ethic includes trying to both be prepared for surprises and to be flexible in your thinking and planning.

Adjusting to the unexpected requires having a plan B whenever possible. Try to always think to yourself, "*What happens if . . .?*" to try to prepare for the unexpected. Contingency plans will help you quickly adjust to whatever curve ball life throws at you. This is particularly important when planning important or significant events or aspects of your life such as financial planning, surprise parties, or work presentations.

It would be ideal if you could plan for all contingencies in life, but that would be impossible. It is for that reason that you need to be flexible. Being flexible will facilitate a speedy and corrective adjustment to unplanned issues when they occur. If you are rigid in your thinking you will keep trying the same thing only to continue failing because it doesn't apply to the situation any longer. If you are rigid in your thinking it will prevent you from quickly thinking out of the box, which is often required when something doesn't go as planned. Collin, a 27-year-old lab tech, is a good example of dealing with the unexpected.

Collin

Collin was hired for his first professional position following a 2-year certification training program in the medical field. Historically, Collin has not managed his time very well. Video game play has been the primary interference with his procrastination of assignments and inability to manage his tasks in a timely manner. Beyond his video game play as an obstacle for his time management, Collin does not judge and plan his time out well at all. Work ethic and time management have been a major clinical focus in his therapy.

Collin's new job, his first since graduating from his training program, required him to be in the laboratory by 8:00 AM. He lived 30 minutes from the lab but a major construction project created a parking problem for the entire facility. The construction required Collin to park offsite and take a 5-minute shuttle, provided by the company, from that parking lot to the building.

The second week into his new job, Collin told me he had been late 3 times already. We examined his morning process and how he was getting ready. I asked him to list all the steps he needs to take to get from his bed to the lab, and calculate the amount of time each step took. When he presented his "homework" to me in the following session, it was a job well done. The problem was, that even though he calculated the amount of time the shuttle took from the parking lot to when he was clocking into work, he was not accounting for the fact that the shuttle is sometime late as much as 10 minutes. There was also one time when he was unable to get on the shuttle because of its capacity and he had to wait for the next one. Collin started to adopt the same defensive attitude as Charlie did when he missed the train. He just became annoyed and believed he was doing all the right things to get to work on time. In fact, he was, but he was not being flexible by planning for contingencies and the unexpected. In his case, it was the shuttle schedule. We explored his options. There were only two he could come up with. One was to pay for a monthly parking spot in a garage that was within 1-minute walking distance to the lab. He rejected that because the cost was prohibitive. The only other option he had was to adjust his timing leaving at least a 20-minute buffer time to account for the shuttle mishaps. Collin did not formulate that conclusion on his own. If he wasn't guided toward more flexible thinking, he would remain stuck and probably lose his job. The train, or in his case, the shuttle, would keep leaving without him. Tom Coughlin, the then head coach of the New York Giants football team told his players, "If you are not fifteen minutes early, you are late." That is an excellent philosophy to live by.

Excellence

Booker T. Washington said, "Excellence is to do a common thing in an un-common way." Being excellent makes you uncommon and special. Working toward being excellent in everything and anything you do will help potenti-ate a great deal of success in your life. Excellence will enable you to make the train more times in your life than not. There is a distinct difference between working toward excellence and working toward perfection. Perfection leaves no room for error while excellence allows for mistakes and flaws. When you work to be excellent you often work toward the ideal with the reality that it may be impossible to attain. That makes us strive toward excellence with the absence of disappointment if we fall slightly short of it. Working toward the ideal helps us to be excellent without the pressure to be perfect. When you strive toward excellence in everything you do, you will always be putting your best foot forward.

Excellence If Far Reaching

When you have a mindset that you need to do everything in an excellent manner, you are setting yourself up for many, many positive experiences, out-comes, and feelings about yourself. A mindset of excellence means that you put forth maximum effort on both small and large tasks insignificant and sig-nificant tasks. Whether you are changing a light bulb in a lamp or performing triple bypass cardiac surgery, it is imperative that you be mindful of every step, never cut corners, and work toward the best outcome. Admittedly, it sounds a little ridiculous with the light bulb changing, but if you are going to do some-thing or anything, do it right. Make sure you have the correct bulb base, the proper wattage for that particular lamp, and screw it in evenly so you don't strip the threads.

When you do things in a consistently excellent manner you will more than likely be viewed as a high quality, competent person. Others naturally flock toward competent people. Striving toward excellence is an attitude and gives you distinction because you will stand out in a positive way. You will have an attitude of self-assuredness, not cockiness. You will have a self-pride of knowing that you are always doing your best. Excellence keeps you focused and motivated on the goal or prize. You will have a vision of winning and a persistent will to win. Keeping excellence in mind with everything you do will keep you determined and make you tenacious. Your motivation will be high and you will know when not to give up, and when to give up.

Mediocrity and passivity will be unacceptable if you adopt an attitude toward excellence in all that you do. It helps you want to be better and prevents you from sitting on your laurels. Working toward excellence means that you will always try to improve and make changes to improve. But, you never feel disappointed in yourself, that you missed the mark, or failed because you know you tried your best and worked toward excellence. You, and no one else, can fault you for that.

Work Ethic

By distinguishing between play time and work time, running your life in an organized manner, and constantly working toward excellence, you can develop a fantastic work ethic. With a great work ethic, you will find yourself running your life instead of your life running you. The amount of stress and crisis occurring in your life will be greatly reduced. A positive work ethic helps you feel on top of things. It enhances the potential for success with both tasks and in your relationships. A strong work ethic makes you a dependable, competent person. It is part of the formula for seeking your happiness, freedom, and self-fulfillment in your life.

The self-discipline you practice contributes to overall healthiness because you will eat better, spend your time wiser, and attend to the small and large demands in your life. Being organized helps you implement your plans and meet the demands in your life in a way that almost runs itself. Being planful and managing your time well makes it almost effortless to do everything you need to do on a daily basis. Strangely, it also creates more free time to do whatever you want to do. The result of leading a self-disciplined and organized lifestyle, coupled with the motivation to always do your best, not settle for mediocrity, and strive toward excellence, will be a great work ethic.

Work ethic runs like a thread in your life that applies to all aspects of your life. Applying a good work ethic to your job, your relationships, your health, and everything and anything you do in your life will pay off tremendously. It is a core attribute that can be applied to execute every triad in a successful manner to lead a happy, free, and self-fulfilled life. A good work ethic will set you up for never missing the train.

By combining the discrimination between work and play time, being organized, and striving toward excellence in everything you do, you will be gaining a significant edge up on experiencing happiness. A good work ethic enhances every aspect of your life. Your day, your work, and your relationships just run smoother when you don't shirk your work, you are organized, and you attempt to be excellent in everything you do.

CHAPTER 9

Problem Solving

Perception*Perspective*Balance

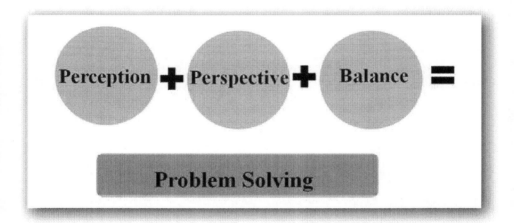

Perception

As you experience the world you integrate all of the information through your senses. Your brain has to make sense of all of the stimuli that enters it, and as it does, it creates your reality. It is *your* reality because everyone does not interpret the world exactly the same way. The way you interpret the information received by all of your senses, sight, hearing, smell, taste, and touch, becomes your perception of the world that you readily accept and act upon. Unfortunately, our perceptions are not always accurate. Even more potentially problematic is the fact that people readily accept their perceptions as truth and conduct their lives based on what they perceive. Our senses can fool us and our brains accept it.

In addition to the commonly recognized 5 senses, we also perceive other stimuli in our environment that are less traditionally defined. Temperature is something we sense and is interpreted by our central nervous system. My father would constantly talk about the temperature of the room or outside. He would repeatedly adjust the thermostat after asking whoever was in the room if they felt cold ... or hot. He would adjust it regardless of their response. His biological thermostat was difficult to regulate, which caused him to focus on the thermal readings of his surroundings.

Time is another perception that alters our thinking, emotions, and behavior. The perception of time can be radically different than the actual time that has lapsed. Sitting in my 50-minute college calculus class felt like 4 hours. When I got married, my Uncle Jesse shook my hand and said, "Congratulations. I hope your marriage lasts as long as mine seems."

Social perception or how we interpret interpersonal interactions and social situations is another nontraditional sense that we have. Misinterpreting communications and social situations can lead to unhappiness, anger, and even embarrassment.

How we see, or perceive social interactions can sometimes be accurate and sometimes be misinterpreted. At the beginning of my career, I was conducting a consult for a school regarding Hector, a 9-year-old boy who was a frequent disciplinary problem in the classroom. As I talked with him, I learned that he often misbehaved at home, as well. He told me that his parents lock him a closet when he would become angry. As a young, probably naïve psychologist, I became upset, even angry with his parents. I decided to meet with them and confront them on their rather inhumane punitive methods. I even surmised that it was possible that Hector's abusive parents were at the root of this boy's acting out. To my surprise, my perception of what that 9-year-old told me was a gross misperception. The parents, being rather sensitive and resourceful to Hector's interest, built him a fully equipped art studio out of the huge walk-in closet in his bedroom. They would often suggest that Hector draw or paint as a way to regain control over his anger when it began to emerge. They were using the room therapeutically, and appropriately, despite both Hector's and my misinterpretation.

Another example of how misinterpretations can lead to anger and embarrassment is yet another consult I was conducting with Adam, a 15-year-old mildly learning disabled youngster, who happened to be an only child. I was administering what is known as a projective drawing test, which, when interpreted, can reveal much about the clinical issues of a patient. The test I was giving him is called the Kinetic Family Drawing, a test to reveal family relationships and family functioning. The directions are, "I would like you to draw every person in your family, in action. Draw each person doing something." Adam became quite uncomfortable and incensed. He refused to do the drawing and became very agitated. I didn't push it and we went on to other things, all of which he was cooperative. Later that day I received an irate phone call from Adam's mother. She told me she was extremely upset with me. I asked her what she was so angry about and she told me that Adam told her that I wanted him to draw his family, which to him, an only child, meant his parents, having sex. To Adam, a hormonally raging adolescent, "in action" was interpreted as drawing his parents having sex.

Reality Checks

Fortunately, in both Hector's and Adam's situations I was able to do a reality check. Reality checks are important because they can help provide you with the appropriate, more accurate interpretation of specific situations. You should be aware of doing reality checks before you actually react to a social situation. It can be difficult to realize when reality checks are needed because your perceptions *are* your reality. But, there are signals to pay attention to such as if something doesn't make sense, or if it seems absurd or extreme, or if your emotions are running high as a reaction to a person or situation.

Reality checks provide you with a foundation for problem solving in your life. In fact, performing reality checks by asking, exploring, and observing, you can eliminate a substantial amount of problems in your life. In the first example, I ended up obtaining a reality check with Hector's parents. That immediately ameliorated my upset and accusatory posture with his parents. In Adam's situation, once his mother understood the actual meaning of the directions of the Kinetic Family Drawing Test, she was able to explain to her son which in turn, abated his anger toward me.

Old Tapes

Sometimes, old tapes create present problems. Perceptions of a here and now experience can be slanted or skewed by issues that have affected you in the past. This most frequently occurs in present day situations that resemble past situations. For example, if a friend of yours tends to lie or exaggerate the great deals she gets on purchases, when she tells you about the "steal" she got on a piece of artwork for her home, the integrity of her story will be doubted due to your learned perception that she often misreports regarding her purchases. I had a couple, Jerry and Linda, in therapy with me and one of Linda's main issues was that her husband was overly flirtatious with women. Jerry was very a very warm, touchy-feely type of guy. They were watching television one night and Jerry's cell phone kept receiving texts. He would read them, chuckle, and then reply. Linda became very angry in session, citing his flirtatious behavior once again regarding the texts received that evening. Her perception was based on previously learned experiences with Jerry, however, the reality was that he was texting with his sister and they were making fun of her husband. Her perception was based on previously learned experiences with Jerry, however, the reality was that he wasn't texting flirtatiously with a woman, he was joking with his sister.

Perceptions can be based on your own issue filters that have nothing to do with a specific individual or similar situation. You may perceive a situation through the eyes of a psychological issue that you carry with you everywhere you go. If you are self-conscious about having a large nose which makes you feel embarrassed, you may believe that others are staring at your nose and only your nose when they speak to you. Your own issue biases you and causes you to distort or misperceive the situation.

Understand And Be Aware

If you understand and are aware of your issues, you can better scrutinize your perceptions. More accurately, understand and *beware* instead of understand and be aware. Misperceptions and distortions cause problems. They can create conflict in your life unnecessarily. There is probably enough conflict in your life that you certainly don't need to add to it by having flawed perceptions. If you are aware of how you tend to "see" things, you can better scrutinize and sift through situations and communications with a more objective eye.

There are usually certain signals that may alert you to perceptions that may be askew. Consistent misperceptions involving the same issue is one way you can second guess your perception of a situation or communication. If you have trust issues, you may erroneously discount true statements or information on a frequent basis.

Keying into your feelings is another way to be aware of a possible misperception. If you feel anxious, uncomfortable, or angry, for example, it might be a signal that you are misperceiving the situation. Your feelings could be based on a reality based situation, as you may be detecting something emotionally before you become cognitively aware of what is causing your feelings. Nevertheless, you need to take inventory and try to ascertain if you perceive the situation accurately or not.

Another method to help you determine the accuracy of your perceptions is to use good old fashioned common sense. If something seems absurd, out of character, or just plain doesn't make sense, it may be that you are misperceiving or misreading the situation. Take a step back and try to think through the situation logically. I always like to ask myself, "If this wasn't true, what could be the alternative explanation?"

Perform Reality Checks

Reality checks were already mentioned above. Checking out what is accurately perceived and what may be inaccurate is key to determining if your perceptions are erroneous or not. You can do a reality check by discretely asking another person who was present to determine if they interpreted it as you did. You can also do a reality check by asking questions to gain more information. The new information you obtain may negate your initial interpretation of the event.

Questioning yourself and trying to approach the event from different angles will help you test the reality of the situation from a more objective point of view. If you try to approach objectivity and fight subjective misperceptions you will avoid difficulties and minimize stress in your relationships. The reality is, if you don't get to the station at the scheduled departure time, the train will leave without you whether you think it will be on time or not. It is best to deal with reality of the train's on-time record as opposed to what you *believe* about when the train is leaving.

Perspective

Whereas perception is the interpretation of a situation, perspective is how you look at it. Is the glass half empty or is it half full? Are you an optimist or a pessimist? Do you expect things to go awry or do you have an image of a predetermined image of a successful outcome? Everything, and I mean everything, is how you think about it from a point of view, or perspective. Even the most horrific circumstances can be muddled through with less problems and stress if you have a positive attitude. My friends, Arnold and Dierdre are perfect examples of, "everything is how you think about it." At age 36 Dierdre was diagnosed with Leukemia-the type that has a high mortality rate. She had 3 young children under the age of 10 years old. Arnold told me how intense the chemotherapy treatments were going to be, and how they would affect Dierdre. I remember the first time I visited her in the hospital, walking out of the elevator and feeling uneasy. Dierdre had just finished her initial intensive round of chemotherapy and I expected a hospital room filled with fear, anxiety, gloom, and one very sick friend. I entered Dierdre's room and she and Arnold were, laughing and joking. They had just ordered expensive steaks from one of their favorite restaurants in Manhattan and they were virtually making it a party in that hospital room with all of her tubes and nausea, and fatigue, and the beginnings of her hair falling out. Arnold and Dierdre know how to deal with problems with perspective-always a positive perspective. In Chapter 10 the effect thoughts and beliefs have on how you feel and act is expanded upon. For now, suffice to understand that your perspective has to do with how you tend to think. Your perspective will either help you with everyday problems or they will bog you down in stress and negativity, depending on what your perspective is in that situation.

Frame Of Reference

The adage, "One person's ceiling is another person's floor" is based on perspective. Depending on your frame of reference, in this case from a physical point of view, the same part of a room will be a floor or a ceiling depending on where you are in the building. Perspective comes from your point of view. Literally, that point of view can be from where you are standing. In terms of seeking happiness, freedom, and self-fulfillment, your perspective will be largely contingent upon your social point of view. Your perspective is affected by previous life experiences, your moral compass, your ideas about ethical behavior, and your self-esteem. You should always be aware of how your perspective affects social interactions, and social conflict problem solving.

Your frame of reference needs to be questioned and challenged when making important life decisions, or trying to solve a problem. Challenging and questioning your frame of reference will give you a broader perspective so you don't become enmeshed with a problem that you are too close to be able to see the whole picture. Your perspective can always be changing and evolving. Your perspective, depending on your frame of reference, can even create good or bad feelings about your life. You can always look at other people's lives in a comparative, competitive sense, and realize how little you have compared to what they have in their life. You can also look at others and be grateful for what you have compared to what they have. You can always look up and you can always look down. But what you should do is just look in the mirror.

What Affects Perspective?

There are several factors that affect your perspective. These factors will affect your overall perspective in life that gets applied to most, if not all, situations. They will also affect the way you are viewing specific situations, as well. You need to consider which ones apply to you, and which ones influence your view of the world. The factors that will affect your perspective are:

- Cognitive Style
- Life Experiences
- Life Changes
- Trauma

Understanding how these factors influence or provide your vantage point will be instrumental in problem solving and facilitating happiness, freedom, and self-fulfillment in your life.

Cognitive Style

Everyone has a particular way of thinking about the world using our thought process. The way we tend to think about ourselves and the world we live in is called your cognitive style. Cognitive style is a consistent thought pattern that you use to process information and apply to most of the situations you encounter in your life. Your cognitive style will be your preferred way of thinking and approaching problems. It is your natural inclination without even consciously trying to approach the problem in that manner.

A common cognitive style is the *all or nothing* thinker. All or nothing thinkers tend to see the world in black and white. Gray is usually difficult for all or nothing thinkers to consider. If you have an all or nothing style of thinking you are more than likely somewhat rigid and regimented in your life. Structure and predictability are comforting to you because the rules are clear and you do not have to adjust or adapt very often. All or nothing thinkers have the perspective of always and never. Without readily recognizing that sometimes things are a certain way, or a person often will behave this way, all or nothing thinkers have an absolute and extreme perspective when it comes to the world and how people act towards them.

Steve is an example of how all or nothing thinking can affect perspective and problem solving. Steve will often become angry with his wife because she *always* leaves him the car with an almost empty gas tank. She *always* forgets to bring his clothes to the dry cleaner. She *never* deposits her paycheck in the bank the day she gets paid. The fact is that Sherry will *sometimes* leave the car almost empty, *sometimes* forget to go the dry cleaner, and *rarely* deposits her check a day later after payday. Because Steve is an all or nothing thinker, when Sherry makes any of these mistakes Steve experiences them as *always*. The feelings associated with always or never are far more intense then the feelings associated with sometimes. Steve's perspective when Sherry makes a mistake elicits a far more extreme emotional and subsequently verbal reaction due to his all or nothing thinking. In social problem solving, all or nothing thinkers often (not always) have trouble compromising.

Fluid thinking is another cognitive style that affects perspective. Fluid thinkers usually have the ability to look at a situation from different perspectives. One thought prompts another, and then another, with a chain reaction of possible solutions or observations. Fluid thinkers tend to be more creative thinkers. Fluid thinkers also have the ability to think in a divergent manner. They can adopt a perspective that most people cannot easily see. Fluid thinking affects perspective both positively and negatively in terms of problem solving. It facilitates creative solutions and problem solving but it also can convolute, confuse, and bog down problem solving because the thought process can be led far astray from the original issue. Sometimes, fluid thinkers can see both sides of an issue so clearly that it becomes difficult for them to make decisions or take a stand.

Linear thinkers have the perspective of a logical and rational world. Linear thinkers view the world as predictable and reasonable. A step-by-step approach to problem solving is utilized, with each step having a logical, common sense link to the previous step. Linear thinkers can be great social problem solvers when logical and rational thinking can apply. Unfortunately, there are many social conflicts that logic and reason just do not apply.

Some people use a cognitive style called adaptor. Adaptors tend to be people pleasers. They try to adapt to the problem instead of formulating possible solutions. Adaptors run into difficulty because the same problems keep cropping up in their lives. This occurs because conflicts are not truly resolved; they are merely placated so they keep recurring due to no change in the precipitating circumstances. The natural inclination of adaptors is to think of most problems as something that isn't important enough to take a stand on. Adaptive thinkers have the perspective of being agreeable to eradicate problems in their lives. Adaptors are often people pleasers, not problem solvers.

Innovators are the opposite of Adaptors. The innovator cognitive style produces possible solutions that no one else has considered. Innovative thinkers tend to look beyond traditional or conventional problem solving strategies and solutions. Whereas adaptors use the given information and adjust to the protagonist, innovators build on existing information and tenets of the problem and create solutions that enable growth and change. In social problem solving, an innovative cognitive style can be quite useful to find solutions that help both individuals feel happy and satisfied with the eventual outcome.

People have cognitive styles that dictate how they tend to think about things. Your cognitive style will be an asset or a problem, depending on the situation and the perspective you take. If you are aware of the cognitive style you tend to use, you can determine if your perspective is accurate and helpful in any given situation.

Life Experiences

Life experiences have an effect on your perspective. How you view yourself and the world can be dependent on the consistent and repetitive experiences you have had in your life. A simple example is a raffle drawing. If you have entered many raffles or random contests in your life and have never once won, when you enter a raffle you will most likely have the negative perspective of, "I'll never win this thing." Your perspective is shaped by the numerous occasions that have had the same outcome. So, when you are encountering a present day situation that is identical or resembles a previous situation, your perspective is altered. When I give presentations and workshops to both lay and professional audiences I almost always receive rave reviews. At this point in my career, my perspective is that I will give a great presentation and receive great reviews. When it doesn't go well, and sometimes it just doesn't, my perspective is shaken and I have an uneasy emotional reaction. It is just not what I expect based on my perspective, which developed as a result of consistent previous successful performances.

Caution should be used if your perspective lies heavily in previous life experiences. Your experiences in the past do not always necessarily mean that the social problem or situation will have the same turnout. If your perspective is tainted, you can alter the outcome simply by your expectation-a form of self-fulfilling prophecy. Years ago I had a 19-year-old patient who inherited, along with his two siblings, 11 million dollars from his grandfather. He told me that he went into a Porsche dealer to buy a 911 which was a $50,000 car at the time. Billy was dressed in typical 19-year-old fashion, blue jeans and a rock group logo t-shirt. The car salesman had the perspective that Billy was just another teen looking to try to get a way to drive a high performance luxury sports car by posing as a customer and asking for a test drive. The salesman was condescending and on the nasty side, giving Billy a negative, dismissive attitude. Billy left the dealership and bought the 911, paid in full, from a competitor. That salesman's perspective, based on previous experiences, cost him a very nice commission on an expensive car.

Life Changes

Significant changes in your life will also create a perspective. The most obvious and significant life change is when you have your first child. I knew my wife for 8 years before we had our first child. When Daniel was a month old, we were sitting at the dinner table, he was thankfully asleep while we were eating, and I turned to my wife and said, what did we used to talk about before we had Daniel?

Life changes alter the way you look at and experience your day to day experiences. They are life altering, making significant and long term changes on your quality of life. Life changes can involve events such as securing a dream job with significantly more salary, winning the lottery, being diagnosed with a chronic ailment, or getting married. Life changes that carve out your perspective can also be gradual changes. Developmental changes, or going through life's psycho-social stages such as adolescence, or senior years, can determine your perspective.

Trauma

Whereas life changes are events that have a long lasting or permanent effect on you, traumatic events are specific episodes in your life with a distinct beginning and ending. However, when they are over, they have long lasting effects that shape or change your perspective. Being in a severe auto accident, a victim of rape, being cured of cancer, and the sudden death of a loved one are examples of traumas that can alter your perspective.

As in most of the other factors that formulate your perspective, trauma can create a negative or positive attitude. It can also help with productive problem solving or be counterproductive in problem solving. Sometimes trauma can cause you to not sweat the small stuff because you realize how precious life and your time can be. It helps you focus on the more important aspects of your life. Trauma can help you take a look outside of yourself, to be more objective and evaluate how you have been conducting your life to make appropriate changes. Trauma can also taint your perspective in a cynical way so that you see life mostly with gloom and doom. Sometimes, trauma occurring to someone close to you can change your perspective. The 911 terrorist attack directly affected thousands of people, but changed the perspective of an entire country.

Reactions

Take a look at what your perspective is and try to determine what the factors are that are shaping it. Perspective is a comparative concept that is relative to your own individual view. Your emotional reaction to people and problems in your life is highly contingent upon your perspective. Consequently, your actions and behavior will follow suit. If you are acutely aware of your perspective, you will be able to reduce the intensity and duration of conflicts and problems in your life. Understanding your own perspective can also help you understand others' perspective. Being able to understand another's point of view will be an instrumental tool in problem solving and building happy, healthy relationships.

Balance

Balance is one of those key words that are used throughout this book, in relation to most, if not all, of the ideas for living a happy, free, and self-fulfilled life. All of your traits, behaviors, social interactions are best when they are tempered with balance. In terms of problem solving, balance is no different. Employing the concept of balance to your social life and social conflicts is instrumental in reducing and solving problems in your life. Usually, too much of anything will more than likely cause conflict and problems in your life. If you are the type of person that likes getting your own way, your social problem solving will be difficult. The lack of balance in acquiescing even when you want your way will cause more friction in your relationships and even destroy some of them. People do not want to be around others who want things and their preferences to excess. It becomes more of a taking than a give and take relationship.

Life Is A Juggling Act

Twenty-first century life is complicated. It is a life filled with complexity and options. That can be a good thing, but it can also be a hindrance to living a happy, free, and self-fulfilled life. Since we tend to have so much and so many people in our lives, and so many activities we engage in, we tend to spread ourselves very thin. Attending to all of the things and people is like a juggling act. Actually, it is more like a plate spinner.

If you are old enough to remember a popular 1960's television show called The Ed Sullivan Show, you will remember plate spinners. The show was a variety show highlighting acts such as musicians, comedians, magicians, dancers, and anyone else that had a talent-or what was considered talent for 1960's television. Periodically, they would have a plate spinner as an act. He had a pole with 6 or 7 tines attached to it. The plate spinner would spin a plate on one of the tines and the centrifugal force would keep it balanced on the tine. Then he would add another plate to a second tine. Then, a third and fourth plate would be spinning. Soon enough, he had 6 or 7 plates spinning simultaneously on this pole with tines. When one plate would lose some of its velocity he would quickly rush over to it and spin it. He needed to continually spin each plate as it became wobbly so that it didn't fall and crash. Yes, this was television talent in the 60's.

You must run your life like a plate spinner. You must attend to all of the "plates" in your life to keep them spinning. When one requires attention, you must attend to it so it doesn't fall and crash. Your plates are your spouse, family, job, extended family, friends, yourself, your hobbies, and anything and anyone else that is in your life that requires your attention. Having balance in your life means attending to all of these entities and not letting any of them crash due to a lack of attention on your part. Look for signs that one of your "plates" needs attention. They are usually there if you pay attention. Maintaining balance in your life will not only help you be proactive and reduce the amount of problems in your life, it will also facilitate quick and effective problem solving.

As you go through your day, week, or month try to take notice of the plates in your life. Look for signs that one of the people or responsibilities in your life is wobbly and in need of attention. Do whatever it takes to bring that feature or person in your life up to speed again so it doesn't come crashing down. Many a divorce is the result of a lack of attention and work in the marriage. I also know many marriages that are more like roommates than romantic partners because they do not attend to one another. Look at your children, your parents, your friends, your colleagues and reach out to them. Take inventory at work and attend to the responsibilities and people if you have been neglecting them. Make sure you pay attention to yourself, as well. Your plate needs spinning at times. Sleep, appetite, concentration, and fatigue issues are signs that your plate is losing velocity.

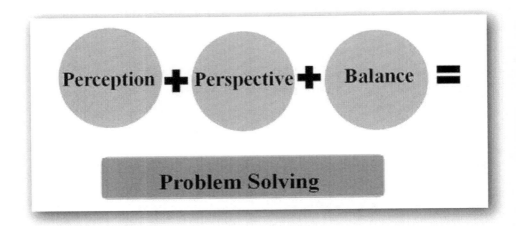

Problem Solving

Everyone has problems. Problems do not know how wealthy or poor you are, how physically healthy or unhealthy you are, or if you are an infant or elderly. Patients come to me with problems. I can help them either solve those problems or help them find better ways to cope with them. When a couple comes to me for couple's therapy, I tell them I cannot eliminate their arguments, but I can help them argue better. In other words, they can learn how to problem solve once they understand their perception of the problem, see their own and their spouse's perspective, and apply balance to the situation.

Since we can't prevent problems from ever occurring in our life, we need to learn how to problem solve. Effective problem solving is part of the formula for living a life filled with happiness, freedom, and self-fulfillment. Once problems are tackled, they don't accumulate and hang on our backs. Unresolved and repetitive problems accumulate inside of us and weigh us down. They cause us to feel fatigue, depressed, anxious, and a lack tolerance. Problem solving involves the triad of perception, perspective, and balance.

Self-Awareness

The first step in problem solving is to become acutely aware of your perception of yourself and the world. You also need to understand your perspective as it applies generally and in each specific situation. Becoming aware of your perception and perspective puts you in an excellent position for creative and effective problem solving. It will allow you to have the balance you need to be able to resolve conflicts with others. Furthermore, having self-awareness enables you to better cope with problems you are having in your life when they don't even involve another person.

Discovering self-awareness involves taking the time for self-reflection. Looking inside of yourself must be done with as much objectivity as you can muster. Your thinking has to be distraction free so find times such as driving alone in the car, lying in bed, or sitting alone in a dark room. Think about what people who are close to you tell you about yourself. Much to your chagrin, they are often correct, although they give you feedback about yourself through their own perception and perspective. Nevertheless, the lens you use to look at yourself should include how others' see you.

Spending time thinking about yourself when you are by yourself is the easy part. The difficulty lies in the moment of conflict or when you need to address a problem in the present. Whenever possible, try to hit the pause button, much like the pause button on a video game. When you hit the video game pause button it freezes the action and gives you the luxury of time to figure out your next move. In the throes of a conflict, whenever possible, try to hit the imaginary pause button to allow you to gain perspective and examine your perception of the situation. That will enable you to create a balance and problem solve.

Listening and paying attention to the person you are having a conflict with is a great way to become aware of your own perspective and perception of the problem. Often, if you let down your defenses and don't stay so entrenched in your own point of view, you can become aware of how your position is contributing to the problem. Grace, a 12-year-old patient with Obsessive-Compulsive Disorder (OCD) is a great example of how considering another's perspective helps you become aware of your own.

Grace was sitting in her science class as her teacher was handing back a test the students had taken the other day. Mr. Margiotta placed Grace's test paper on her desk, as he was doing for every other student in the class. Grace promptly threw the paper on the floor, got out of her seat, and scrunched under the desk, refusing to come out. Mr. Margiotta didn't really know what was going on, but Grace was prone to acting out and being belligerent on several other occasions. Grace's bizarre behavior triggered his teacher authority posture. Grace wouldn't budge so he called down for the crisis intervention worker, who promptly came and was able to remove Grace from the classroom. On the surface, this teacher-student conflict looked like a student behaving inappropriately, perhaps as defiance toward authority or perhaps for peer attention. The teacher, needing to gain control of the situation and maintain control of his classroom, invoked his authority. The result was a standoff and escalation of the problem.

When I was processing this incident with Grace in session the following day, I was able to unveil the real issue for Grace. She told me that before the teacher placed the test paper on her desk, he licked his finger to separate the pages easier. Her OCD kicked in big time, reacting with fear and anxiety at the prospective germs now contaminating and swarming on her test paper. Out of fear and panic Grace reacted the way she did. It wasn't defiance or peer attention as Mr. Margiotta assumed. If he immediately became aware of his own belief that this was a threat to his authority and put it aside for a moment, he could have asked Grace about how she was feeling and why she had behaved in such a bizarre manner. Instead, he instantly treated it as belligerence. If Mr. Margiotta had paused for a self-awareness moment, he may have gotten past his own perspective of teacher to student and dealt with Grace as a youngster in distress.

Coping Mechanisms

Humans have a strong need for self-preservation of our self-esteem. From an extremely young age we begin to develop different ways to deal with and defend against real or perceived emotional attacks to our self-esteem. If we find some success in using a particular coping mechanism, we tend to use it and overuse it. In the end, coping mechanisms can be very helpful when dealing with problems in life. However, we usually don't stop there. Most people misuse coping mechanisms so that they actually perpetuate the problems or conflicts instead of helping us guard against them. There are many types of coping mechanisms but the most common forms of defense mechanisms are:

- Denial
- Rationalization
- Minimization
- Displacement
- Reaction formation

Denial occurs in two very different ways. When someone accuses you of something that you are actually guilty of, you deny responsibility. This type of denial is conscious and purposeful and we call it lying. The second type of denial is more of a psychological process. Denial as a psychological defense mechanism is not only lying to the accuser, but you are also lying to yourself. This type of denial hides the truth about your actions from yourself and can be very destructive in problem solving. If you do not take ownership for a mistake, then you would have no reason to change your behavior or resolve the issue with the other person. This ends up with lingering anger and sore feelings for both of you because of the lack of resolution. Denial is never a productive defense mechanism for problem solving.

Rationalization is a defense mechanism that attempts to justify your actions to yourself and others. It makes you believe that whatever you have done wrong is justified because of one or more reasons. Rationalization is also used to ward off bad feelings about yourself. If you tend to use rationalization as a defense mechanism it can either be helpful or destructive to problem solving. Rationalizing an inappropriate action will certainly not help solve your dilemma or enhance your happiness. Your doctor tells you that you need to lose 25 pounds so you go on a diet. You are doing really well on that diet for 2 weeks and have lost 7 pounds. A cheesecake is placed in the break room at work for all who want it. You rationalize that it is okay for you to have a piece because you have been doing so well on your diet for 2 weeks. That is the beginning of your downfall for the quest of losing 25 pounds. On the other hand, rationalization can be a helpful tool in problem solving. Your wife's 40th birthday is in 3 months and you want to take her away for the weekend. Funds have been somewhat tight so you begin to feel anxious about spending the money for the getaway. So, you begin rationalizing to help you allay the anxiety and solve the problem. The two of you have not been away together in 3 years. It is a special birthday for her and your holiday bonus was a bit more than you expected. Both of you have been feeling like you are in a rut and a weekend away could really create a rejuvenating feeling for both of you. Rationalizing in this case will bring happiness for you, and resolve an issue at the same time.

Minimization is a way to make something seem less upsetting. By reducing the importance or magnitude of a problem or emotion it makes it seem less intense. If you tend to overreact or frequently look at the worst case scenario, minimization can help put your feelings and reactions into perspective. On the other hand, if you minimize something that is far more serious than you consider, you will not deal with the problem effectively.

Displacement is when you blame others for your wrongdoing as a way to protect your self-esteem. Instead of taking responsibility for your actions or the problem, you make it somebody else's fault. Remember Charlie, the victim of the irresponsible train? His first statement to me was, "My Monday morning class professor is failing me." The inference in that statement is that it is the professor that is doing it to him. He went on to blame the train engineer for "leaving without him. Charlie uses displacement for many of his mistakes in life. How can he improve and be happy, free, and self-fulfilled if he never needs to change himself?

Deflection is a form of displacement. When you deflect you are passively and subtly not taking responsibility for your actions. Deflection is probably more commonly experienced and used by you than you realize because it is so subtle. An example of deflection is when your wife yells at you for being late again without calling for the third time this week and you respond, "All you do is yell at me!" Another common example is when you tell your 12-year-old to clean her room for the fourth time today and she responds, "You are always nagging me!" Or, when your friend is annoyed that you forgot to pick up the cake sale leftovers and you respond, "Come on Beth, you are always forgetting things. All three responses shirk your ownership in the problem and displace it elsewhere. Problems will not be solved if you continue to deflect.

Reaction formation is a way of coping with unpleasant feelings or situations. Reaction formation occurs when you adopt the exact opposite feeling or thought from your original feelings and thoughts about a specific situation. You do this as a way of saving face and convincing yourself that you really don't care that much. Here are two examples of reaction formation used by an employee and a teenage boy.

Lois, an assistant manager of a major pharmaceutical store chain was up for a promotion to store manager. Lois very much wanted this new position and the raise that went with it. When she found out that she was passed up her immediate reaction was to tell her husband, "I didn't want that job anyway because this is terrible company to work for." She coped with her disappointment by trying to convince herself that she didn't want the job at all.

Lance, a 15-year-old had a crush on the girl that sits in front of him in Geometry. He kept telling his friends how pretty she was, how nice she was, and how smart she was. Lance became friendly with her by talking to her before and after class, and walking down the hall with her. His friends kept bugging him to ask her out but he was too nervous to do so. He finally got up enough courage to ask her to hang out with him. She told him that she recently broke up with a boyfriend and she wasn't interested in going on any dates right now. When Lance's friends asked him how it went he told them she turned him down, and that it didn't matter because she is such a bitch anyway. Lance needed to get angry with her to deal with his hurt and rejection. Using reaction formation as a coping mechanism he adopted the exact opposite feeling to the real feelings he was experiencing.

There are several important things to remember when thinking about coping mechanisms. You should try to recognize when you are using them, and which defense mechanisms you are using. Next, you want to evaluate whether or not you are using them effectively in problem solving situations. Using defense mechanisms judiciously and at the correct time and place can actually help solve your problems while maintaining your self-esteem.

Using The Triad

Problem solving is a skill that, when learned to accomplish effectively, is an essential part of living a happy, free, and self-fulfilled life. By recognizing your own perceptions and perspective in various problem solving situations, you will be able deal with many of those curve balls life throws at you. By balancing where you are at with regard to the problem with other perspectives, you will increase your chances of coming up with a positive solution. It is equally important to detect when your perceptions are inaccurate so that you can change your perspective.

Balancing your reactions which are determined by your perspective and perceptions will complete the three dimensions needed for effective problem solving. Learning from your mistakes and generalizing them to new, but similar situations, will help expedite future problem solving. Remember-your goal cannot be to never make mistakes because that would be impossible. Your goal in life is to try to not make the same mistake more than once.

CHAPTER 10
Coping With Stress
Thoughts*Emotions*Behavior

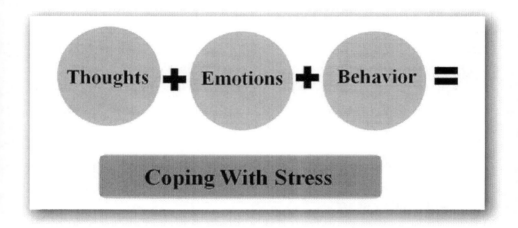

Thoughts

At the risk of repeating myself, it all begins with thoughts. One of the most important distinctions between humans and all other living things is the fact that we have a mind that can think, contemplate, analyze, process, remember, and generate new thoughts. Other animals do show planning behavior and seem to have memory. But their minds do not generate the sophisticated complex thought structure using language as human beings do. Our minds run the show when it comes to how we navigate through life.

If you have had the pleasure of raising a child from birth, you can practically see the mind growing almost daily in the early years. In infancy, it seems that as each week goes by your baby is learning new behaviors. He or she starts to feel a sense of efficacy in having an effect on the environment and begins to contemplate, plan, and predict reactions. As language and thoughts develop even further, a set of core beliefs begins to unfold within the mind of a child. Through repeated accumulated experiences children begin to formulate thoughts and beliefs about themselves and the world around them. The most significant thoughts and beliefs become a set of core beliefs that creates feelings and dictates behavior. Your core beliefs set the stage for your entire life. Core beliefs actually run your life, but the interesting thing about them is that you do not consciously think about them. They are ingrained in you and are always with you, determining how you act and cope with life's stressors.

Your core belief system, although rooted in childhood years, does change throughout adulthood as new encounters and life situations are experienced. Your beliefs can be lumped into either adaptive beliefs or maladaptive beliefs. Adaptive beliefs are the cognitions and belief system that help you be successful, happy, and keep you safe from physical and emotional danger. Adaptive beliefs are true, logical, real, and helpful. Examples of adaptive core beliefs commonly held by people are:

- I am a good person
- If I work hard I will usually be successful
- People treat me well
- I can trust people when they earn my trust
- People respect me
- People generally like me
- I am deserving of being loved
- I cannot remain in toxic, unhealthy relationships

Maladaptive beliefs are cognitions that are unhelpful, illogical, irrational, and false. Examples of maladaptive beliefs are:

- I am not a worthy person
- I should trust everyone
- I should trust no one
- I am entitled to get things even without working for them
- I am unlovable
- People tend to reject me
- I am not intelligent

Adaptive Beliefs

Adaptive thoughts help us feel good and guide our interactions with the world. They are healthy and keep us healthy because they generate emotions and behavior that guide us toward happy, free, and self-fulfilled lives. Adaptive thoughts help us maintain perspective and help you interpret the world more accurately relatively free of skewed negative filters. You are able to do so because adaptive thoughts are true, realistic, and rational. If you believe you can trust people while using scrutiny, you can easily tell when they are trying to manipulate or dupe you, and when they are sincere and genuine.

Since adaptive thoughts are part of your core belief system they are unconsciously present. It would be a great idea to take some time and try to write down your adaptive beliefs about yourself, your relationships with people, and your general abilities. Adaptive beliefs are positive, helpful, and healthy so you want to hold onto them and try to use them in your daily dealings. Because adaptive beliefs are helpful in your life, they help create success and positive experiences and relationships. In this sense, they become self-reinforcing in a positive way. Adaptive beliefs should be maintained and not be changed. Adaptive beliefs keep us motivated toward successful relationships and task completion. They help steer us in the right direction, make good decisions, and regulate our positive behaviors to improve our overall functioning.

Maladaptive Beliefs

Maladaptive cognitions are harmful to your self-esteem. They make you feel badly, hold you back in work and personal relationships, and cause dysfunction. Maladaptive thoughts and beliefs are also not within our awareness, yet, they have a major impact on how you feel about yourself, your relationships, and your competence. Negative thoughts and beliefs prevent you from coping with stress. They prevent you from taking risks and often create a set of social and occupational behaviors that create problems for you in your life. Just as adaptive core beliefs are positively self-reinforced, unfortunately, maladaptive beliefs become self-reinforcing in a negative way. If you have a core maladaptive belief that people are always out for themselves and don't consider you and your needs, then you will treat them with a certain amount of contempt and mistrust. This may cause you to keep people at a distance and inhibit you from giving in your relationships. Consequently, you will not become close to others and they will not go out of their way for you because they do not get anything in return in the relationship. Thus, the belief that people are always out for themselves and not there for you is reinforced.

Maladaptive beliefs need to be challenged and changed. You must first recognize the core set of maladaptive beliefs you possess, and determine the irrationality and falseness of them. By examining the evidence of reality testing you can begin to challenge maladaptive beliefs. I had a 20-year-old patient who came out to me about his sexuality. Raj was terrified that his parents would find out. He was born and raised in the United States but his parents were born and raised in India. Being gay in India is forbidden, unacceptable, and illegal. Raj's belief was that his parents would disown him, stop loving him, and be angry with him because he believed they were rigid, conservative, and close-minded about progressive social views. We broke down their relationship and he saw how much they truly loved him. Raj recalled several examples during his adolescence that his parents became open-minded and flexible despite their own very different adolescent experiences in India. Raj was a typical American teenager regarding his clothing choices, hair styles, and activities that expressed his identity. Despite being completely alien to his parents, they allowed him to experience and choose many of these identity expressing experimentations. The evidence was stacked enough for him to challenge and overcome his misbelief that his parents would react completely negatively and horribly. We decided to have a session with them so I could be a support for him. Although his parents were shocked, they were quickly accepting of his homosexuality. They had many questions, but they were all asked with the goal of trying to understand it, not challenge it, deny it, or change him. Raj developed the maladaptive belief that his parents were rigid and conservative because of numerous experiences he had had with them, as well as numerous comments they have made regarding specific social issues in the news and among their social group. If he did not challenge the belief that his parents are rigid and stuck in their traditional Indian culture, he would have experienced much conflict and stress hiding his homosexuality from them.

Emotions

Humans and other animals are able to experience feelings, are aware of feelings, and are able to express feelings. What sets us aside from other animals is our ability to identify what we are feeling and clearly communicate them verbally. If you have ever owned a pet you know that animals do express their feelings verbally, but it has to be interpreted. When my dog, Bailey, who is completely deaf since birth, needs something he makes a howling noise. But, he makes that same howling noise when he is hungry, wants to be walked, or wants his favorite toy that is stuck somewhere that he cannot reach. We have to interpret his feeling of minor distress in that moment, sometimes by trial and error. To some degree, people are similar because we don't always express our feelings clearly and accurately. We also don't express our feelings verbally. Feelings are often manifest through behavior or somatic complaints, which will be discussed later in this chapter.

Emotions, and the human capacity to be aware, identify, and experience them in a sophisticated manner often run your life. It is your affective, or emotional world that is the determining factor in your ability to experience happiness, freedom, and self-fulfillment in your lives. It is feelings that are the true glue to satisfying relationships, and having positive relationships set the stage for overall happiness. Your feelings actually run your life so it is important to understand them and figure out how and why you feel a certain way in specific situations and with specific people in your life.

Stress And Feelings

Stress is experienced through emotions. It is a pressure felt sometimes as if your head feels like it is going to explode, and other times it is your whole body that feels it. Experiencing stress is tantamount to feeling it. It is the feeling you get when you experience stress that enables you to identify your distress. The most common feelings associated with stress are anxiety, depression, pressure, panic, overwhelmed, and frantic. At the root of what you feel is what you believe about the stressful situation you encounter. Stress and stressful situations do not create feelings. It is what you believe about those specific stressful situations that creates your feelings. Your ability or inability to cope with those feelings is both the true source of your stress and the determining factor as to how well you handle stress. Consequently, your ability to cope with stress becomes paramount in determining your feelings associated with that particular stressful situation.

Behavior

The third dimension in Coping With Stress is behavior. Behavior is simply how we act. Behavior is distinctly different from thoughts and emotions in that it is completely observable to others. Even if your behavior is not obvious, such as not paying attention to a conversation, others will still experience your behavior. Thoughts and feelings are internal and hidden from others. Other people only discover what you think and how you feel as you express it behaviorally. As discussed in Chapter 4, you communicate your thoughts and feelings in two ways. They are expressed either verbally, using spoken or written words, or nonverbally, using behavior, behavior patterns, and body language. Despite your ability to communicate what is going on inside of you to others, it is always up for interpretation. Even if you are clear in verbalizing your thoughts or feelings, as you learned in the previous chapter, the person on the receiving end may have a different perception of perspective from your true intention of the message. Expressing your thoughts and emotions through nonverbal behavior is usually less clear than verbal expression, and even more open to interpretation.

Verbal Communication

Talking and writing what you think and feel is considered to be a behavior. Despite the risk of misinterpretation, the clearest means of behavioral expression of thoughts and feelings is through verbal communication.

Merely expressing yourself verbally is not enough. Communication also involves a listener who determines if the message was received as you intended it to be meant. By measuring the person's response to what you say, you can gauge how accurately they received your message. You can then modify or reword your message so that they have a better understanding of what you are trying to convey. Even if your words are misinterpreted, if you are addressing stress and problems that crop up in your life using verbal language, your chances of coping effectively with them increases markedly. Verbal messages are less prone to misinterpretation than other behaviors that you exhibit, making them the most effective means of coping with stress. The source of stress, as well as the potential solutions to relieve stress can be directly resolved.

Nonverbal Communication

Nonverbal communication encompasses body language, body movement, and behavior patterns. Again, it is believed that 60% of the true message that you send is sent not through your words, but through your actions and body language. Nonverbal communication includes tone of voice, word emphasis, volume, facial expressions, body posture, hand and arm gestures, and any other body movement that sends a message. Nonverbal communication also takes on the form of behavior patterns.

At the beginning of therapy, Chip made offhand comments about the fee. He stopped mentioning the fee but began forgetting his checkbook. He was always on time for his appointments, did not forget or miss any appointments and seemed to be a well-organized individual. He did not complain of being forgetful and boasted about being a detail oriented person at work which helped him be successful. His behavior pattern of intermittently forgetting his checkbook was a nonverbal message expressing his anger at having to pay the therapy fee. This was confirmed when I confronted him which allowed us to resolve the issue. Once we discussed it and came to a resolution, Chip never forgot his checkbook again.

Nonverbal cues connected with verbal statements can completely change the entire message of the actual words. You can say, "Can you please pass the butter?" in a soft and pleasant tone of voice. Those same words, "Can you please pass the butter?" spoken in a loud, sharp tone emphasizing the word, "PLEEEAAASSEE" will communicate impatience, anger, and exasperation. Each statement, even though the words are exactly the same, communicates a different message and will elicit a different reaction.

The major problem with nonverbal behavior is that it is up for interpretation. Interpreting someone's behavior can be difficult and filled with error. If you walked into my office and saw me sitting in my chair crying, what would you surmise that I was feeling? Possible interpretations of my crying behavior are:

- Maybe someone I cared about just died so I am sad
- Maybe someone made me so angry that it brought me to tears
- Maybe I was feeling so lonely

- Maybe I was laughing at something so funny that it made me cry
- Maybe I was thinking of something sentimental
- Maybe I was trying so hard to repair something that it made me frustrated
- Maybe I have terrible allergies
- Maybe I was peeling an onion

I could be feeling any one of those feelings. You would not know unless you actually asked me, but if you walked out of the room without asking me what was going on you would walk away with your own interpretation and assumption of what was happening for me.

Your behavior is just the top layer that is observed by others. There are layers of thoughts, emotions, and motivations that drive that behavior. If you start a conversation with a colleague and they avoid eye contact, give minimal verbal responses, and quickly find ways to stop the conversation, you may read these behaviors as her disinterest in socializing with you or becoming friendly. In reality, she may experience a great deal of social anxiety and would love to become friends, but her anxiety prevents her from engaging in conversations with you. In this case, you walk away feeling rejected, and she walks away feeling embarrassed.

The New Nonverbal Communication

A new form of nonverbal communication has emerged in our digitally driven technologically saturated culture. It is the nonverbal message that is embedded in our computer mediated communication (CMC). CMC includes texting, emailing, social media posting, chat rooms, website boards, and any other written communication using computers and devices. Nonverbal messages accompany CMC communications in the form of written expression just as they do with all other verbal communications. The following are examples of CMC nonverbal communication:

- Capital Letters-when a text or post is written in capital letters it is emphasizing or shouting out the words.

- Response Time-the amount of time a person responds to a CMC may be sending a message. Responding immediately may mean attentiveness and interest, while taking a long time to respond may be expressing anger, annoyance, or disinterest.
- Omission-if a group text leaves you out it may be saying something about the group's feeling about your friendship. Also, if a picture of several of your friends is posted in social media with a caption about how great the party was (that you didn't know occurred), there is a message about their desire to include you in social gatherings.
- Frequency of Contact-how frequently someone contacts you may be an indication of their dependency on your relationship, or a great deal of interest in maintaining your friendship. It is a statement as to how important you are to them.
- Innuendo-sometimes CMC messages allude to specific subjects without really stated them directly. For example, your friend, who is angry with you about cancelling dinner plans posts a picture of her dog Chloe on Facebook and states, "Chloe is a woman's best friend."
- Font- a change in font in terms of type, size, color, bold, and italics may be sending a nonverbal message depending on the verbal content.

The interesting thing about nonverbal behavior is that the message is sent and it is usually experienced subliminally. You receive the message, it doesn't consciously register, yet you respond to it as if you are completely aware of the nonverbal or behavioral message. That makes nonverbal behavior extremely influential in your relationships as well as in your ability to cope with stress.

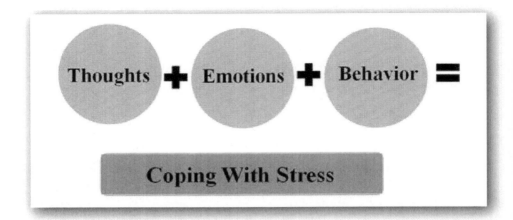

Coping With Stress

Stress is part of life. Show me someone who has no stress in their life and I will show you a bored, lonely person. If you are participating in life in a meaningful way, stress is likely to accompany even the most fulfilled life. The goal is not to eliminate stress and conflict from your life, but it is to reduce the frequency, intensity, and duration of stressful situations. You must learn to deal with stress effectively if you don't want the train to leave without you.

Stress is experienced differently by different people and is manifest in many different ways. The telltale signs that you are experiencing undue stress in your life are through somatic complaints such as headaches, gastrointestinal complaints, and a compromise of the immune system relating to infections and systemically related illnesses. Stress is also manifest through behaviors such as avoidance of responsibilities, spinning your wheels and not completing tasks. A sign of stress can include sleeping difficulties such as insomnia, intermittent wake states during the night, or excessive sleeping. Fatigue, either physical or emotional is yet another sign. There are also cognitive indicators that you might be experiencing stress overload. Cognitive indicators are associated with difficulty with concentration, an inability to sustain your focus and concentration, obsessive, repetitive thoughts, or a foggy feeling in your head. Yet another sign of stress is addictive behaviors such as the excessive use of substances, video games, shopping, gambling, or just about anything that you may be using to channel or escape your feelings associated with stress in your life. Interestingly, addiction is not only a sign of stress it is also a way to deal with it, albeit harmfully.

Minimizing Stress In Your Life

There are many things you can do to minimize stress in your life. One of them is to read this book in its entirety and use the ideas presented. This book provides you with a framework to live your life under control while maximizing happiness and thereby reducing stress. At the very beginning of this book I made mention of my gifted mentor's advice to run my practice and not let it run me. That is a metaphor for living a happy, free, and self-fulfilled life so that the train does not leave without you. The very thrust of this book is to have you control and run your life instead of your life running you. In doing so, not only will the train not leave without you, you can catch the train you want and have plenty of relaxing time to spare while waiting for the train to arrive.

Incorporating a good work ethic, sustaining positive social relationships, feeding your own self-esteem, being observant of your own life, and being planful will help minimize your stress. Attending to the details in your life will also prevent small problems from becoming huge problems. I had a patient who came in for his appointment one day, extremely angry and stressed. He had ignored one of those little red warning lights that pop up on the dashboard of your car. He kept putting it off thinking that the car was running fine and there were no unusual noises coming from the engine. So, he let it go. He finally took it in for service only to discover that the red light was a low oil indicator. His engine was slowly leaking oil from a loose cap, which did considerable damage to his engine. What could have been a 5-minute servicing with a $4.00 quart of oil put in his engine turned into a 1 week $5000.00 servicing. There are often red flags, or signals, that you are beginning to experience stress. Identify what those are for you and try to attend to them as soon as possible. That way you may be ambushing a $5000 service in your life by paying only $4.00.

As stated earlier, you can minimize stress but not eliminate it from your life. There are a variety of ways people cope with stress. Some people have developed appropriate and helpful coping strategies and others use inappropriate and harmful means to cope with their stress.

The ABC's Of Coping With Stress

Each dimension of the *Coping With Stress* triad has been described as part of the formula for dealing with life's nuisances and pressures. Thoughts, emotions, and behavior have an important interrelationship with one another. Understanding their relationship is a large part of learning how to cope with stress.

There is a fundamental strategy that you can use to deal with the stress in your life regardless of the source. I call it "The ABC Method." The "A" stands for affect, or feelings, "B" stands for behavior, and "C" stands for cognition, which are thoughts and beliefs. There is a direct relationship between your thoughts/beliefs, your feelings, and your behavior. Your thoughts and beliefs about yourself and the world create your emotions, as well as your behavior.

Cognition (Thoughts And Beliefs)

Everything starts with cognition. As it was discussed earlier, our thoughts and beliefs about yourself and the world are embedded within you. Some of these beliefs are positive, realistic, true, and helpful in dealing with life and stress. Others are negative, false, unhelpful and maladaptive. Whatever you think or believe about a person, a situation, or even yourself in relation to your stress is the core culprit causing the stress as well as the remedy to relieve your stress. As mentioned previously in this chapter, your core belief system has its roots in childhood. However, it doesn't stop changing and modifying into adulthood. Many of your core beliefs are automatic. You are certainly aware of the feelings and behaviors you experience associated with stressful situations. But, you are usually not aware of your beliefs about the situation. Since beliefs drive the feelings and behavior, the first step in coping effectively with stress is to identify the automatic core belief that may be causing the stress related feelings and behavior. Your thoughts and beliefs create your feelings in relation to that stress. It is a linear relationship whereas thoughts cause feelings that are manifest through behavior. Many common core beliefs are a result of some of the defense mechanisms discussed in Chapter 9. Maximizing, minimizing, denial, rationalization, and displacement are some of the defense mechanisms that plague maladaptive beliefs about stressful situations. Examples of core beliefs that may be at the root of your stress, or even causing your stress, are as follows.

- I am not as good as her/him
- I am not worthy of love
- I am not deserving of success
- I always mess up
- Things always go wrong for me
- I am an unlucky person
- People don't like me
- I can't get things done on time

The above are examples of automatic, maladaptive, unhelpful beliefs that are certainly operating but not within your awareness. They both cause stress in your life and are the keys to coping with your stress.

Affect (Emotions)

Feelings are a result of your cognitions. Feelings are created by what we think and believe about specific situations. For example, if you believe that you do not know the material well for a presentation at work, then you will feel anxious about giving it. That presentation, as the actual date lingers, will cause stress because you believe you will do poorly. If you believe that your vacation to Spain will be fun and sensational, then you will feel excited about going. If you believe that terrorists might attack Madrid while you are there, then you will feel nervous about going. Beliefs create feelings. Good feelings and bad feelings.

It doesn't matter if your belief is true or not. It will still create your feeling. If you believe that you could have a heart attack when it rains, then whenever it rains you will feel scared, worried, and nervous even though rain has no rela-tionship to heart function. Perhaps two family members died of heart attacks on rainy days.

Behavior

Behavior is simply your actions. Behavior is directly observable to yourself and others. What makes behavior a different component from thoughts and feel-ings is that behavior is not hidden. Behavior can be misinterpreted because it is a manifestation of thoughts and feelings but since thoughts and feelings are hidden behavior must be interpreted in terms of what you are thinking/believ-ing and feeling in any given situation. The ironic thing about behavior is that it can reverse the linear relationship so that the behavior, which is manifest due to the feelings which are caused by the belief. These behaviors resulting from thoughts and feelings can reinforce the feeling you have and support the belief that started the whole mess in the first place. Sounds confusing? It is circuitous whereas the belief causes the feeling and the behavior, which in turn maintains the bad feeling and results in the belief becoming reinforced. Still confused? Take a look at this example.

> **Belief:** I am an imposter at work. My colleagues think I am great at what I do but I really don't know what I'm doing. I've been fool-ing them all along and eventually they will find out the truth about my skills.
> **Feeling:** Anxious and worried that I will eventually be found out.
> **Behavior:** I hold back, lack aggressiveness, turn down challenging projects, and don't allow colleagues to get too close to me.

Over time, the following occurs.

> **Behavior:** I keep holding back, do not assert myself, do not go after high profile projects, and I set up firm boundaries with my colleagues and bosses so they can't learn about the "real, inadequate me."

Feeling: Anxious and worried that they are going to "find me out."
Belief: Because I put up barriers to my success, I do not advance. This reinforces my belief that I am inferior to my colleagues and they will discover the real me.

Most often interpretations of behavior are accurate but sometimes they are not. It is not unusual for you to overgeneralize your core beliefs and apply them to situations when they really don't apply. Julia and Paul discovered that phenomenon first hand.

Julia And Paul

Julia and Paul entered couple's therapy with me at Julia's strong urging. She believed that Paul was extremely controlling of her and it caused many conflicts in their relationship. Julia felt like a "second class citizen" in the marriage, having to comply with Paul's demands and opinions about how they should conduct their lives and parent their 2 children. Julia often fought back and attempted to assert herself but felt very ineffectual in their marriage and in the family. Paul agreed to counseling because he recognized that they were battling on a frequent basis, sometimes over relatively inconsequential issues.

The couple worked hard in therapy, and to Paul's credit, he began to relinquish control and started giving Julia more credibility in her opinions regarding decision making for them and the family. Just as they were beginning to make progress, they began one of their weekly session with a lot of anger toward one another. Julia accused Paul of reverting back to his old controlling ways. When asked how this was being manifest, she talked about his request for her to curtail her credit card spending and reducing the amount of cash he would give her each week for food and miscellaneous family needs. Julia viewed this as Paul using money to revert back to his controlling ways. Paul, in turn, was angry about Julia "withholding sex" as a way to respond vindictively.

As it turned out, Paul explained, and reminded Julia, that he had been discussing the difficulties he was having in his business for the past few months.

He had been making a comfortable living enabling Julia to be at home with the children. Historically, money had not actually been a control issue in their relationship because there were never any financial concerns. Adding to a drop in business, a key employee left his firm and took several large clients with her, limiting Paul's income even more. What Paul was asking in cutting back in Julia's spending was based on the reality of their new financial situation. Julia erroneously applied the old control issues in their relationship based on her belief that Paul was controlling, despite the fact that it was a logical, pragmatic adjustment to their lower income. Without realizing it, her automatic belief that her husband controls her, Julia became angry and fought back with passive-aggressive behavior using withholding of sex.

Using the ABC's To Battle Stress

Effectively dealing with stress is a 4 step process and it begins with your thoughts and beliefs.

1. The first step is to recognize your unique signs and symptoms of stress. As discussed earlier, those signs can be emotional, physical, or cognitive by way of attention, concentration, obsessive, and unclear thinking. Think about your unique reaction to stress when you are not feeling stressed, so that you can quickly identify the signs. The faster you recognize that you are experiencing stress, the easier it might be to alleviate it.

2. Once you realize that you are stressed, try to identify the thoughts and beliefs that are driving your stress reactions. Most often, these thoughts are not true, are illogical, or too extreme. At the very least, even if your thoughts are accurate in applying to the stressful situation, it will be helpful to identify them.

3. After you become aware of the negative or maladaptive thoughts that are at the root of the stress, challenge them with positive, reality based statements. Search for the evidence that helps you combat the bad thoughts and turn them into positive self-statements.

Ask yourself, "Is this real or is it being magnified inside my head? Is it logical? What is the worst case scenario? How is my belief affecting my emotions and behavior associated with that stress? Here are some common beliefs often associated with stress and how to challenge them.

I am never going to get all of this done.
"I usually get everything done, and I'm never late. I can always put some due dates off for some of these things to give myself more time."

I will not be able to meet my monthly bills this month.
"I will do the best I can and pay as much as I can. I will make it up next month by working overtime, as I have in the past."

I have too much to do and too little time to do it.
"I can prioritize and rearrange my schedule. I have done this successfully in the past. Not everything is imperative to get done in this time frame."

I will not be able to give that presentation in front of all those people.
I will not make a fool of myself because I know my material. I have done many presentations before and they were well received."

4. Finally, after you have become aware that you are stressed, have identified the thoughts driving the stress and then challenged them with positive self-talk, you make a plan. Sometimes merely making a plan and seeing that you are capable of dealing with the stressful situation is enough to relieve your stress. Implementing a well thought out plan will undoubtedly alleviate or eliminate your stress.

There are certain stressful times in your life that you are unable to change or develop a plan to deal with the stress. In these situations, you simply have to tell yourself that you will do the best you can and that has to be good enough. Acceptance, on both an intellectual and emotional level will not change the circumstances but you will not feel as emotionally drained or distressed.

As you identify your belief systems and thoughts in different situations, the trick is to hold onto the helpful, true beliefs and challenge the unhelpful, irrational beliefs. Challenging and eventually changing irrational thoughts enables you to take control and do something about the source of the stress. Once your beliefs are positive and realistic, your feelings change to more positive or relaxed emotions, and finally your subsequent behavior changes.

Remember, you have the power over stress by the way you are thinking about it. You can either help or exacerbate your stress based on your thoughts about the situation. The ABC's of dealing with stress are augmented by the concept in the previous chapter about problem solving in your life on maintaining perspective. Emotions help you lose perspective, causing more intense emotions. Get a handle on what you are thinking and you can handle your emotions more effectively.

PART THREE
Making It Happen

CHAPTER 11

Competence

*Strengths*Weaknesses*Efficacy*

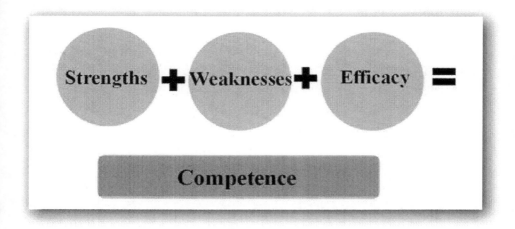

Strengths

Strengths are specific qualities or traits that you possess. Your strengths can be thought of in two ways. The first type of strength is associated with physical qualities such as artistic, musical, athletic, and intellectual, to name a few. Physical strengths tend to be more observable and recognized in our culture. They can be quantified or measured.

As discussed in the chapter on *Identity*, the other type of strength is associated with personal strengths. Personal strengths are not as visible, observable, and easily measured as physical strengths. Nor are they often publicly rewarded or acknowledged with medals or awards. These strengths have to do with your personality traits, how you treat others, your integrity, and your character. They are like the wind. You can't really see the wind, just the evidence of its presence. You can feel it and experience the effect it has on trees, objects, and even the air temperature (wind chill temperature).

Physical Strengths

Most physical strengths originate with your brain wiring. We all enter the world with neuro-biologically predetermined proclivities for specific temperaments and potentially exceptional skills. Naturally, if they are practiced they become a strength. The point is that if you don't have that predetermined aptitude for a specific strength or skill, no matter how much you practice you probably won't become exceptional at it. You can certainly make it a strength in your life, however, it will never come naturally and effort will always be needed to maintain it as a strength.

Examples of how these attributes are acknowledged are awards such as an actress receiving the "best actress" Academy Award, the Most Valuable Player in Major League Baseball, Valedictorian of the class, or even getting the game ball for the winning hit, or a medal for first place in a 100-meter freestyle swim meet. These are public acknowledgements that validate competence and self-worth. When you exhibit them consistently, they become a strength. When you receive positive feedback from others regarding your successful escapades and accomplishments, you incorporate that information into a positive self-esteem.

Personal Strengths

Also discussed in the chapter on *Identity*, was the "non-specific factors" occurring in the therapeutic process that potentiate a positive therapeutic outcome. These "non-specific factors" that occur between the therapist and patient include the patient's perceived interest, attention, and degree of caring demonstrated by the therapist. When present, these attributes have been found to be as important in determining a positive therapeutic outcome as the actual therapeutic technique used by the therapist. Non-specific factors in therapy are more difficult to quantify and measure, just as personality traits such as being a natural leader, kind and caring, respectful, considerate, determined, hard-working, or an empathic individual are difficult to measure. Just like the wind, only the evidence of these traits can be experienced. They are subtle, yet of utmost importance.

The subtlety of personal strengths needs to be recognized and acknowledged even if they aren't as obviously revered in our society. Personal strengths become strengths when others provide positive reinforcement for their existence. Social reinforcement gives personal attributes and skills validity and credibility. But again, sometimes they are not overtly recognized by others, despite the fact that they are valued. The work environment is no different. That employee that pays attention to details to avoid big mistakes and save company money is extremely valuable but her attention to detail is not really measured or acknowledged. The receptionist in the law firm mentioned earlier, that greets and treats each client as special and important does not directly account for the billable hours, but does make an important contribution to the overall experience of the client. The managing partner does not equate her personal strength to the bottom line of the law firm. The manager who keeps employees happy so that they remain invested, loyal, and productive is as important as the money that group makes for the company. Yet, he is reviewed and evaluated yearly based on the gross income his group generates.

Take a look at yourself and others in your life and acknowledge the important traits that really make a difference and impact others in a positive way. Acknowledge the effort instead of the outcome, the way others are treated instead of how attractive they are, give the game ball to sportsmanship, and the award for "The Most Benevolent." Taking these traits for granted does not enhance self-esteem and self-worth, yet they are so critically tied to your happiness. Acknowledging them places value on them so that you and others can realize how you positively impact others in a way that lasts a lot longer than receiving the award for "Best Salesman of the Year."

Having personal strengths is far more integral to your happiness, freedom, and self-fulfillment than having physical strengths. Sure, physical strengths will feed your ego and self-esteem. But true happiness, freedom, and self-fulfillment will come from personal strengths.

Weaknesses

Similar to strengths, weaknesses come in two forms as well. Physical weaknesses and Personal weaknesses are juxtaposed to strengths. Physical weaknesses are observable and often measurable. Personal weaknesses are subtle and the evidence of their presence is only witnessed as a consequence-once again, like the wind. Examples of physical weaknesses are exactly the same as the examples for physical strengths. You can have poor athletic ability, little artistic ability, never be "salesman of the year," or never be eligible to take an advanced math class in high school. Personal weaknesses also qualify as the same traits as personal strengths. However, that is where the similarity ends.

As mentioned earlier, personal strengths often go unnoticed or unappreciated. They are somewhat invisible and are usually not acknowledged or easily visible by people and as a society as a whole. That tends not to be true of personal weaknesses. When someone is considered to be uncaring, disrespectful, inconsiderate, lazy, narcissistic, and without conscience, it doesn't go unnoticed as easily as personal strengths do. For some unknown reason, people tend to take positive personal attributes for granted, while strongly reacting to negative personal attributes.

Regardless, it is important for you take inventory of your physical and personal weaknesses so that you can begin to accept them intellectually and emotionally. You want to be aware of your weaknesses so that you can use them to help yourself. Instead of being a hindrance or obstacle in your life, it is possible to either improve your weaknesses or compensate for them.

Efficacy

Regardless of your particular strengths and weaknesses, how you use them determines whether or not you are effectual as a person. How effective you are in your interpersonal, family, and occupation is highly contingent upon how you use your traits. To be a happy, free, and self-fulfilled person you must be a person that gets things done, gets them done consistently well, and goes through life in control. It is the type of control over the tasks involved in running your life, as well as self-control over your thoughts, emotions, and behavior. An efficacious person doesn't allow the train to leave without him or her.

An efficacious person makes sure they get to the train station on time, and does so without a frenetic, chaotic, and stress filled journey.

Efficacious People

Efficacious people get things done without a lot of tumult or struggle. They are task oriented individuals who are organized and utilize their strengths very well. Weaknesses are well managed in efficacious people. Their strengths and weaknesses are used in accordance with a plan of action. Efficacious people execute. They are pleasant to be around both socially and occupationally. Personal traits that are common among people who just seem to be on top of their lives is that they are usually comfortable with themselves, have self-confidence, and just seem to always be on top of things. Confidence is tempered, not grandiose or arrogant. They usually have leadership qualities and are expected to fulfill the leadership role by others. Effective people approach tasks with a positive outlook and will persist at tasks and relationships to maintain and improve them. Success is their vision and failure is taken in stride. Their efficacy is built on acknowledging previous successes, both large and small. Improving your efficacy in daily tasks, relationships, and at work generates more internal motivation and drive to be even better. The only problem with being an efficacious person is that efficacious people tend to be exploited. Who is your boss going to go to for that extra job that needs to be done by Friday? The efficacious employee or the one that drags his feet, procrastinates, and puts forth minimal effort?

Ineffective People

Ineffective people, on the other hand, do not exude confidence, nor do people usually have confidence in them. Ineffective people usually do not capitalize on their strengths, and often allow their weaknesses to dictate their life.

There are often mini and major crises occurring in ineffective people's lives. They fly by the seat of their pants, and are not prepared for life's twists and turns. It is very difficult to feel happy, free, and self-fulfilled when you are frequently putting out fires occurring around you because of your ineffectiveness.

Ineffective people find themselves treading water instead of swimming and getting somewhere. They often remain stuck in their lives just trying to make it through the day. Fatigue often plagues ineffective people because of the undue stress experienced in their daily activities, and the drama frequently occurring in their relationships. Ineffective people very often miss the train. Even if they make it, they are stressed and exhausted while on the train because of the amount of energy and consequences that poor planning incurred in order to get to the train station on time.

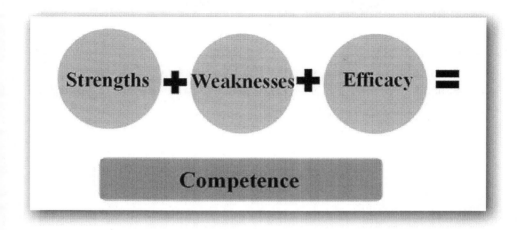

Competence

Competence is not a skill. It is a state of being. For competence to lead to happiness, freedom, and self-fulfillment it has to be how you are, not what you can do. Competence is an attitude-a positive attitude toward yourself. It is an attitude and a belief that you project to others as well. Competence is the result of utilizing your strengths, weaknesses, and efficacy. It is not just having strengths, weaknesses, and efficacy. Your competence will be perceived by others by the way you handle your strengths, weaknesses, and efficacy.

Consistently competent people exude capability, moxie, and a certain amount of know-how in a variety of situations. Others are attracted to competent people. Competent people are usually viewed as leaders, and are often looked up to as a leader. When I was doing my training in graduate school I had a course called Group Psychology. At the end of the 7th class meeting the professor instructed us to meet in a different classroom the following week. He gave no reason for the classroom change and he said that no matter what, every student needed to stay the entire class. That no one was allowed to leave before the usual class time ended. I remember that it felt very mysterious. As it turned out, the classroom was a small theatre in the round. The stage had several cameras in place around the periphery. The seating area was dark with lights focused solely on the stage. The only thing on the stage was about 12 randomly placed chairs (there were about 14 of us in the class). There was no professor. As it turned out, it was a specific group psychology exercise created by the Tavistock Institute to determine how roles develop in groups. The ambiguity of the situation where we were faced with 2 hours of no leadership, no task other than to remain until the class ended created interesting interactions among the students. Leaders and followers emerged but I distinctly remembered how several students felt anxious without a structured plan or specific goal for the class. They readily latched onto and followed the emerging leaders of the group. Even though there was no specified task to accomplish, the people exuding competence and confidence were readily followed by many members of the group.

Developing Competence

To develop a sense of competence you must understand your strengths and weaknesses, and how to use them effectively. The first step is to become acutely aware of your strengths and weaknesses. But remember, it is not as simple as knowing what your capacities and limitations are. It is also learning how to use them effectively. Having valuable strengths alone is certainly not enough to develop competence. Just take a look at the countless professional athletes, successful musicians, or actors who have skills that dwarf most other people on the planet. There are numerous examples of how they became incompetent, losing all of their fame and money, due to poor moral judgment, drugs, or illegal activity.

Competence comes from a continual examination and processing of your daily interactions with others and your responsibilities. Ask questions such as,

"What worked and why?"
"What didn't work, and why?"
"Did I accomplish what I needed to today?"
"What would the people I interacted with say about me today?"

Competence is developed by analyzing both your successes and failures. Competence comes from and is shaped by both successes and failures.

Successes are great, and it is obvious how they can develop your competence as a person. But competence also comes from struggles and adversity in your life, if you use them efficaciously as a learning tool. Be careful not to fool yourself. Sometimes, strengths are illusions. I am sure you know people who think they are much better at something than they really are. Grandiosity is a peril to developing competence because the strength you believe you have is not reality. The difference between self-aggrandizing and competence is that competence is real and self-aggrandizing is merely a defense mechanism to cope with feeling incompetent.

Once you have a clear understanding of your strengths and weaknesses, and you accept them both intellectually and emotionally, you can develop your competence by gravitating toward specific people, tasks, and leisure activities that will provide you with the opportunity to display or utilize your strengths efficaciously. People, tasks, and leisure activities that accentuate your weaknesses need to be avoided when possible. But, it is not always possible to eliminate people or activities that tend to elicit your weaknesses. Developing competence is learning how to either strengthen your weaknesses, or learning how to compensate for them. By surrounding yourself with people and technological devices to compensate for your weaknesses, your competence will improve. When you can, try to avoid or go around people or tasks that tap into your weaknesses. Gravitate toward people and tasks that will showcase your talents and best qualities.

Rhinda's Weakness

Rhinda, a 34-year-old patient is an example of how to compensate for a weakness that became an increasing demand in her job in the market research department of a large clothing manufacturer. Rhinda is very smart and knows market research extremely well. Her ideas were insightful and her reports were exemplary. Both skills were clear strengths for her and helped her experience much success in her job. She was viewed as a competent person at work. As is common, competent people, especially in the work environment, are asked to do extra jobs and relied upon more than incompetent people. As a result, competent people are taken advantage of and exploited by colleagues because they will get the job done and done well. With her increasingly positive reputation, it became difficult for Rhinda to make her meetings on time. Her boss happened to be a stickler for being on time, and held it against employees that were late to meetings. Rhinda had difficulty juggling her usual duties in addition to the special requests people starting making of her due to her dependability and competence. She decided to set her cell phone, which was always with her, to a 10-minute audible alert immediately upon learning of a meeting she needed to attend. She used her third appendage, her mobile phone, as a means to compensate for her tardiness for meetings.

Strengths And Weaknesses Are The Same

Strengths and weaknesses are really the same. They are the same because they are all grouped into skills and personal qualities. In the end, they are all traits. The determining factor, which is really how effectively you use your strength and weakness traits, depends on how you use them, when you use them, with whom, and how often. For example, you can be a positive leader or you can be a bossy person. It is the same trait but it becomes a strength if you use it judiciously and in an inspiring way, and it is a weakness if you tell people what to do frequently and by barking out orders. There are times when it is better to be a soldier and situations that beg you to be a general. Recognize which is which and that determines if that trait is being used as a strength or a weakness. With whom you use the take charge skill also determines if it is a strength or not. You can take control over a meeting with peers if it looks like they need guidance and direction, just as several of us did during the Tavistock experiment. But you can't do that when your boss is attending the meeting. If you are taking control too often, your leadership strength becomes a weakness.

Developing competence involves the ability to efficaciously and judiciously use your strengths and weaknesses. Be aware of each situation using your traits in an appropriate manner, at the right time, with the appropriate person, and not too frequently.

CHAPTER 12

Working Your Comfort Zone

Staying Safe*Stretching It*Leaving It

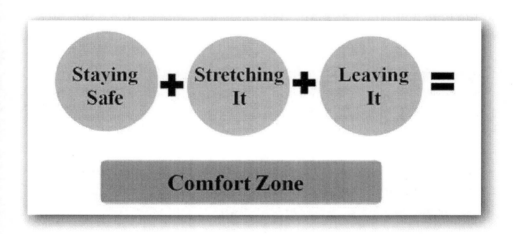

Staying Safe

f you don't want to miss the train, and want to live a happy, free, self-fulfilled life, there are times when you will need to play it safe. Playing it safe means that the train you could take may not be the best train to take due to the potential risk in riding that train. It means waiting for the next train because it is a safer and adequate train to take. That train may not be the most comfortable and may not be scheduled to get you to your destination with a lot of time to spare, but it is much more reliable with an on-time record than the other train.

The reference to "safe" has to do with risk management in your life. When you manage risk in your life you are considering the gains and losses in terms of your feelings and your relationships. You are also mentally examining the cost-benefit in engaging in specific activities and relationships. Sometimes, the wisest thing to do is to play it safe and not take social or emotional risks. The first step is to determine if you should play it safe or not. To do so, you must carefully assess the situation and all the factors and variables that are involved. You must also examine your motivation or reasons to play it safe rather than take a risk.

There are several reasons to play it safe with specific situations and relationships.

There are also the wrong reasons to play it safe which usually ends up in missed opportunities or negative outcomes.

Assess The Situation

When you are faced with a situation or are in a relationship that has the potential for risk, either emotionally or socially, you need to take a conscious inventory of the factors and variables that are associated with that situation. It is similar to the decision making process involved in a business transaction such as buying or selling stock, or whether or not to make a major purchase. You must consider the up-side and the down-side in either going ahead with it or passing up the opportunity. Questions such as:

"What do I hope to gain by doing so?"

"What do I potentially lose by doing so?"

"This may be a good thing for me but is it the right time?"

"Do the gains outweigh the losses significantly enough?"

By asking these questions, and any other questions that are important for that particular situation, you are challenging yourself to think as objectively as possible. This needs to be an intellectual exercise, not an emotional one.

Emotions only cloud your decision making process. I realize it sounds very clinical, perhaps even cold if it is a relationship issue you are contemplating, but it really needs to be assessed similar to a business transaction. If you love sushi and always wanted to own a lunch truck, you cannot buy a sushi lunch truck for $400,000 when it has only netted an income of $35,000 a year for the past 5 years. Your love for sushi and excitement of owning something you always dreamed of cannot enter in the decision making process because it is a bad business decision. In this case it would be wisest to play it safe.

Each situation you contemplate, each relationship you evaluate in terms of its value to you, playing it safe is an option. Playing it safe means that you avoid risks with regard to that situation or relationship. It means that, in your assessment, it is too risky to engage. Staying safe means that you maintain the status quo, but only if your present position is a positive, comfortable one. Inherent in assessing the situation to determine whether or not you play it safe is also determining whether you play it safe for the right reason or the wrong reason. The right reasons have to do with cost-benefit, timing, and amount of risk.

Cost-Benefit

Cost-benefit is usually associated with financial or economic decision making in business. But, the concept can certainly be aptly applied to life decisions, especially when it comes to deciding what to do in social or emotional situations. Cost-benefit involves weighing the down side of doing something against the potential gain. You would be surprised, by consciously doing so, how obvious certain decisions become by actually playing it safe, maintaining the status quo, or avoid delving into a situation or a relationship. Making an actual plus and minus list and assigning a value to each item ranging from 1-10 will facilitate a decision using cost-benefit analysis. The following example entails a decision as to whether or not Simon agrees to re-enter a relationship with Celia. They dated for 1 ½ years and Simon ended the relationship 2 months ago. Celia is now asking him to reconsider and date her again. What would you do if you were Simon?

Benefit/Up Side	Value/ Importance	Cost/Down Side	Value/ Importance
Love	10	Argumentative	9
Companionship	6	Overly critical	9
Have fun together	7	Unreliable	10
Share interests	6	Can be clingy	10
Great sex	7	Controlling	10

The positive aspects of Simon's relationship with Celia are all positive and of significant importance to Simon. However, when he examines Celia's negative personality characteristics and places high value on them, the negative far outweighs the positive for him. He did not renew his relationship with her.

Timing

There is a saying, "timing is everything." The timing needs to be considered in determining whether or not you play it safe. Sometimes the timing of when to do something is the only reason for playing it safe. Maybe it is an opportunity that is worth taking but you have too much on your plate at the time. Or, whatever is being presented to you is attractive but you are in an unstable or sensitive emotional place in your life. The timing is just not right despite the desire and motivation to leave your comfort zone. It might be the kind of thing that you do at a later date. If it is not the right time and you need to play it safe, it might take a bit of self-discipline and restraint. Temptation makes it difficult to deny yourself something that changes your status quo just because it isn't the right time. If the timing isn't right, you should play it safe. Zena is an example of playing it safe due to poor timing. She was recently diagnosed with breast cancer and was undergoing chemotherapy and radiation therapy. She tolerated it well, and the cancer was responding positively. In the midst of her second round of treatment, she was offered a promotion to a job that she very much wanted. The job was challenging and she did not have the appropriate educational training but her bosses thought she could do it. However, it entailed immediate travel and markedly more pressure. She declined, as the timing was just not right.

Amount Of Risk

When the amount of risk far outweighs the gain you should play it safe. Although this seems similar to the cost-benefit analysis it differs in that cost-benefit compares the potential gains vs. the potential losses and amount of risk just looks at the degree of potential damage. Sometimes you might determine that there is just too much to potentially lose by engaging in an activity, changing your job, or making that large purchase. If you are not willing or able to handle the worst case scenario, then it might be prudent to play it safe in that situation.

Playing it safe isn't necessarily a negative thing to do, even though it might have a negative connotation. It is a positive move to maintain the status quo if the loss is just too great for you to handle. Have you ever watched a game show where the contestant has to decide whether or not they should go on and risk losing the large sum of money they have already won? Or, do they risk losing all of it if they botch that next question? Then you know what it means to play it safe due to the amount of risk by going forward and not playing it safe.

Wrong Reasons To Play It Safe

There are also the wrong reasons to play it safe. If you play it safe due to fear, then you are allowing fear to rule your life. That will prevent you from doing things that facilitate your happiness, freedom, and self-fulfillment in your life. Making decisions out of fear will usually end up with the train leaving without you. Sometimes, fear can be a good reason for playing it safe, but only after it is determined that the amount of risk just isn't worth doing it.

Playing it safe because you feel guilty is another wrong reason to play it safe. Feeling guilty is based on the belief that you will do something bad or wrong if you don't play it safe. Many parents make parenting decisions out of guilt instead of due to good judgment. Guilt, like fear, will cloud your objective judgment and interfere with your ability to accurately assess using cost-benefit analysis or ascertaining the realistic amount of risk. Feelings like fear and guilt cloud and distort the thought process and preclude the use of your intelligence as a decision making asset.

Stretching It

Stretching your comfort zone means you are taking some degree of risk. When you take a risk you leave your comfort zone. If you have decided that you are not going to be playing it safe, it means that you are doing something that has some risk and it causes you to enter into the unfamiliar zone. The unfamiliar zone can be anxiety producing and quite uncomfortable. The unexpected accompanies stretching it.

Leaving your comfort zone and taking a risk does have potential disadvantages. Before doing so, hopefully you apply the same process of assessing the cost-benefit, timing, and amount of risk involved in making the plunge into the unknown. Stretching it and leaving your comfort zone is a necessary part of your life if you want to live a happy, free, and self-fulfilled life. Remember taking risks, aside from the potential loss, has potential gain. Those gains, whether they are financial, quality of life, or relationship gains, enable growth in your life. Growth means improving to a better place than you were when you started.

Usually, when you take a risk there is a certain element of excitement and intrigue. Risks can also imbue mystery, glamour, and piquancy. A little seasoning and excitement can go a long way in improving yourself. This makes stretching it, when it is the right time and the correct amount of risk, a good thing to do in your life. Taking too many risks will push the odds that the worst case scenario will occur so make sure you are judicious with your decisions to leave your comfort zone and take risks. I believe that inherent in our DNA, as we progress developmentally through life, that we are meant to grow and change. Taking risks is part of the process to help us improve ourselves. It is what we are meant to do. So, in the words of Albert Einstein, "A ship is always safe at the shore-but that is NOT what it is built for." You can play it safe all your life and never stretch it, but that is not your destiny. That will keep you in the harbor all your life and never discover new lands, new oceans, new people, and new experiences. Living a life filled with happiness, freedom, and self-fulfillment will require risk taking and leaving your comfort zone when it is prudent to do so.

Leaving It

There are times when you play it safe . . . and there are times when you stretch it. You may use the most careful judgment and pragmatic decision making process to do one or the other. You may avoid making the decision for the wrong reasons and make it carefully for the right reasons. Regardless of the decision, it might turn out to be the wrong decision. It is at that time that it is time to simply leave it.

There will undoubtedly be times that you must cut your losses and withdraw from the situation or relationship. This is often difficult to do because you most likely put a great deal of time, money, or emotion into your decision to either play it safe or take a risk. Leaving it requires the same type of self-discipline that staying safe or taking risks does. Perhaps it takes even more because of all the personal investment you put into it.

Leaving it is determined by the same process used to decide whether or not you are staying safe or stretching it. You first assess and then do the cost-benefit, timing, and amount of risk it takes if you remain in the situation. Also similar are the right reasons and the wrong reasons for leaving it. The right reasons are determined through your careful assessment as you are involved in the situation or relationship. The wrong reasons are associated with fear and guilt.

Leaving It With Simon And Celia

Let's take a look at Simon and Celia again with regard to the decision to stretch it or leave it. Should Simon get back with Celia? If he did, he would be stretching it. Clearly, he had some reservations about returning to the relationship. There were reasons he broke up with her the first time, as indicated in the down side of the list. But, careful analysis of the important value a relationship with Celia offers him vs. the parts of the relationship he dislikes helps him make the decision to leave it. He does love her, and there are things about her that he really enjoys, including spending time with her. However, the turn-offs in her personality including her overly critical, controlling, and clingy nature supersede and outweigh the positives. He did consider the fact that those traits could be worked on and improved, but he wasn't willing to put the time in and work that hard at a relationship at this point in his life. Consequently, he painstakingly decided to leave it. Living a happy, free, and self-fulfilled life means eliminating those things, activities, and people that do not contribute positively.

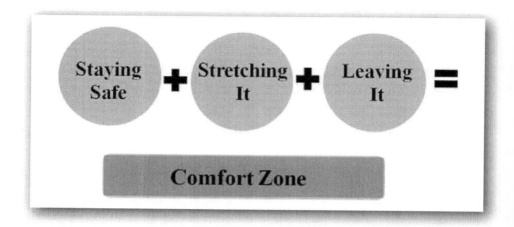

Comfort Zone

Living a happy, free, and self-fulfilled life is not just about eliminating that which does not contribute positively. It is also being able to maintain the positive situations, things, and people in your life, keeping them in your comfort zone. Beyond eliminating the negative and maintaining the positive, you need to seek new situations, things, and people by broadening your horizons and stretching your comfort zone from time to time.

Going through your life and making good decisions as to when you need to play it safe, when to take a risk, and when to leave something is a skill that you will need to continually hone. If you start thinking about the people in your life, your situations such as your job or living situation, and the things you have in your life in terms of making a decision to play it safe, stretch it, or leave it, you will increase the amount of positive aspects in your life. It is a way to minimize the effects of feeling trapped, remaining in bad situations and relationships, and becoming depressed and stressed.

The interesting thing is that if you are carefully making these choices, you end up feeling that you are in your comfort zone almost all the time. The fact that you pensively contemplate when to maintain the status quo, when to take a risk, and when to withdraw from a situation makes you feel comfortable and confident with your decision. Your comfort zone continually becomes redefined because you are almost always comfortable with your what you are doing with your life because you are controlling your life instead of your life controlling you. Even though Simon was initially conflicted about getting back with Celia, which is not a good feeling, and he was initially distraught after he told her, Simon quickly became comfortable with his decision because he knew it was the best thing to do. Taking control over your life, not letting the train leave with you, is making these types of decisions.

CHAPTER 13

Achieving Success

Education*Intelligence*Social Respect

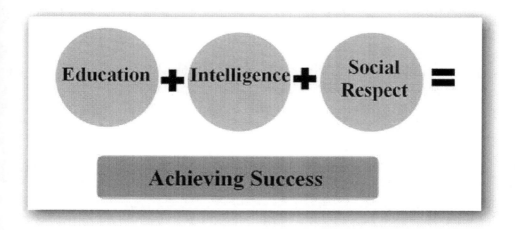

Education

Throughout your life, education occurs both formally and informally. Formal education is when you attend a class, workshop, or program of study to gain information or skills. A formal education is usually pedagogic, didactic, demonstration, or actually executing the skill such as an apprenticeship or internship. In the United States we have compulsory education until age 16. Almost all Americans experience some sort of formal education.

Without realizing it, all Americans receive an informal education. Informal education occurs in a less structured classroom. The classroom is the social environment. Informal education is pervasive and is delivered in a subtle manner instead of a formal curriculum. Learning is strictly in-vivo, that is, on the job or in the social world. You are not graded for your informal learning as you most often are in formal educational situations. However, you are most certainly evaluated – not by a report card-but by the consequences of how you use the knowledge you acquire informally. Learning factual information and skills presented in formal education can also be learned informally, in life experiences. In addition to specific information and skills, informal learning primarily includes life lessons, interpersonal skills, relationship skills, moral development, and overall character development.

The Importance Of Education

Whether you learn formally or informally, or most likely, both modalities, education is essential. It is not only essential for living a successful life, it is essential if you want to live a happy, free, and self-fulfilled life. George Washington Carver said that education "unlocks the golden door of freedom." It is one of those rare things that is both a tool and equipment at the same time because it provides you with a foundation to achieve success. Learning gives you confidence and a sense of competence.

Learning opens your mind. Someone who is not learned or willing to incorporate new ideas into his or her life will be stagnant and lack the ability to adapt to the ever changing world, culture, and their relationships. Education gives you the ability to think critically, make judgments, analyze, process new information, and make good decisions. Information is powerful and enables perspective and the ability to break down problems and situations using prior knowledge. Education builds on itself because you use what you have learned to learn something new. Learning and knowledge provide you with the ultimate freedom which is the freedom to think. People can steal your car, use your things without your permission, and get into your space but no one can take your inner thoughts and ideas away from you. Education also keeps you open to new experiences, which is also a key element to achieving success in your life. New experiences lead to new opportunities.

Education Is Everywhere

Education and acquiring knowledge should never stop throughout your life. It doesn't matter if you are 9-years-old or 90-years-old there is always something new to be learned. At some point in your life formal education usually stops. There are adult education classes and classes for retired people even offered at the college level. But for the most part at some point in your young adult life your formal education ends, whether it is high school, vocational technical school, a certification program for a specific vocation, college, or a graduate degree. When it ends, your informal education becomes the only way to learn for the rest of your life.

Once you have completed your formal education you must continue learning within your social experiences. With the real world as your classroom, to continue educating yourself you need to observe, listen, inquire, and practice new skills. Never be afraid to ask questions. Sometimes it is smart to just sit back, observe and listen to others. Watch what they do, how they act, how they conduct their lives. Formal education feeds your mind, but informal education feeds your morals, your character, the richness of your relationships, and your occupational success. In many ways, your informal education is far more valuable than your formal education. When I interview for a new psychologist to join my practice, I place more emphasis in my decision on their personal characteristics than their knowledge of clinical and therapeutic concepts. My thinking is that if they have learned enough to be admitted to the very competitive Ph.D. program, earned the Ph.D., successfully survived their clinical residency, and passed the licensing exam, they probably have enough education to be a great psychologist. But what they couldn't learn, and can't be formally taught is their ability to connect with others in a warm, genuine, and caring way. They can't learn in a formal educational environment how to handle their own emotions when treating a patient. They can't learn all of those non-specific factors I referred to in Chapters 7 and 11 that are involved in the therapeutic relationship.

Knowledge and information accumulated informally during your life experiences are, in many ways, more valuable than what is acquired in a formal training program. Formal education may provide you with facts and know-how, but your informal education helps you know how to use them successfully and productively. You can be a master cabinet maker, creating the most elegant and perfect kitchen cabinets, but if you don't know how to deal with customers or fellow employees, you will never reach your potential. Not learning about how to deal with people, acquired only in your informal educational environment-living life-will surely hold you back and cause you to miss the train.

Intelligence

Education gives you the tools and equipment, whereas intelligence helps you decide how to use it. If you don't want the train to leave without you, you need to use your intelligence wisely. With the goal in mind of living a happy, free, and self-fulfilled life, intelligence must incorporate a broad definition. It is not strictly your IQ, or how book smart you are. The type of intelligence that you need to use in your life has an expansive definition. It does include your ability to properly use what you have learned in school, but it also applies to your social intelligence. The ability to utilize what you learn in your social environment is largely contingent upon your social intelligence. Using your social intelligence is far more important than your ability to create algorithms or write a financial analysis.

Social intelligence has to do with your adaptability to the world around you. If you have the ability to quickly read situations and people, you will be able to interact in a positive manner. The ability to navigate successfully in the social world, which includes the work world, includes the ability to negotiate, adjust, and intervene appropriately and effectively. You can easily see how social intelligence is an integral aspect in achieving success in your life. I have had countless young patients who struggled in academia. I would tell their parents that we just have to get them through school because their youngster will excel in the world once they are out of the formal learning environment. These students are better at being a student of life than being a student in the classroom. They have high social and moral intelligence and once they hit the streets instead of the books they become very successful. They just know how to handle people and situations in a way that creates success and productivity.

Using Intelligence

There is a difference between being intelligent and being smart. Being smart is the ability to use your intelligence effectively, whether it be high cognitive functioning or whether it be social intelligence. Using your intelligence means to process situations and interpersonal interactions using analytic skills, problem solving skills, reasoning it out, and using logical, common sense thinking.

By applying these processes, you will be able to navigate and negotiate your social and occupational worlds quite effectively. Be adaptable and flexible in both your thinking and your actions. Try not to be right, but be smart. Know when to intervene and when not to put your two cents in. Learn how to get people to listen to you by being judicious with your ideas. Gain the respect of others by being smart enough to know what you don't know. It is very dangerous when someone doesn't know what they don't know. Understand your limits and it is okay for people to know them. If you are smart enough to tell them you don't know the answer to something, when you do offer a solution they will tend to respect it and accept it. Don't try to fake it and don't try to impress people with random facts or sophisticated formulations. When I was doing my clinical training, I was supervised for a year under a Harvard University trained clinician. She was one of the brightest people I ever met yet she rarely used a word longer than 5 letters. She was smart enough to know how to simplify things so that it was relatable to me and everyone she interacted with.

Using your intelligence is to think smart. Try to predict what will happen next so you can be prepared for most situations. Thinking on your feet is a skill that most of us do not possess. Contemplating several possible scenarios and having a response ready to go will serve you well in achieving success.

Using your intelligence means that you are setting goals for yourself. Make them reasonable and meaningful so that you maintain your motivation. Living an intelligent life incorporates long term goals, short term goals, small attainable goals, and lofty dreamy goals. But the one goal that should dictate every aspect of your life is not to make mistakes. That is impossible. The one goal you should always keep in mind is to never make the same mistake twice. Many people, very intelligent people who aren't very smart, keep making the same mistakes repeatedly. There are relatively small mistakes such as getting parking tickets by not feeding the meter, to more upsetting mistakes such as having repeated romantic relationships with substance abusers.

History is the best predictor of the future. Using past experiences, both identical and similar, will help guide you through your job, your relationships, and making decisions for how you live your life intelligently. Instead of using a patient example, I will use myself.

Dr. O

I hate shopping for clothing. I despise it. My wife loves it. She is the best person I know at a lot of things but she is truly the best shopper I have ever met. I have a generally easy-going temperament and usually go with the flow-except when I have to shop for clothes. As soon as I enter a clothing store I start yawning. It's like an allergy. (Or, maybe Pavlov's dog). After a short time, I start to get impatient and irritable. In an effort to expedite the process my wife tries so hard and she sets her targets with the eye of a sharp shooter in picking out articles of clothing for me to purchase. This went on for years with both of us dreading going shopping for clothes for me. I could go myself but I wouldn't end up going at all if it was left up to me. At some point I decided to use my intelligence and learn from the past. My irritability would invariably cause bad feelings between us so I consciously decided to keep my cool, remain pleasant, and not be argumentative. Using my shopping history, I smartly started controlling my demeanor whenever we went shopping together. My wife, on the other hand, also used her intelligence by connecting with a personal shopper, Liz, who has gotten to know me, my taste, and my price range. Prior to our arrival, she has everything all ready for us to consider, knows her stock, and gets me in and out in an hour while outfitting me for the entire season. By the way, Liz is a life-saver. She is one of those people that has the right combination of personality, sense of security, and a marvelous work ethic that creates an air of competence.

Social Respect

Mutual respect was discussed as a triad dimension in Chapter 5 as part of having positive relationships. The dimension of Social Respect as part of your goal of achieving success in your life has to do with conducting yourself in a way that you are respected. Being respected by others should not be confused with being liked by others, having others agree with your opinions, or having authority over others. Social respect refers to how others view you in terms of your integrity, morality, character, and the respect you have for yourself.

When people have respect for you they tend to treat you in a more positive, caring way even if they don't like you or agree with your position. Having others respect you removes the barrier that is created by disdain and negative feelings in the relationship. When you conduct yourself in a respectful manner and treat others with respect, you may not eliminate conflict in your relationships but it will decrease the emotional intensity of the conflict and tend to promote resolution. It is easy to see how important it is to have social respect from adversaries and people that are not fond of you as a component in achieving success in your life. It is equally, if not more important, to have the respect from the people in your life that genuinely care about you and mean something to you. Having social respect from friends, family, and co-workers that do think positively of you is not a guarantee or automatic. Someone can like you, like spending time with you, find you fun and funny, and care about you deeply, but they still lack respect for you. Having all those positive feelings toward you is great to have, but if they don't respect who you are those relationships will always have a barrier. This is closely connected to the trust issue in relationships, also discussed in Chapter 5.

A Two-Fold Process

Achieving social respect is a two-fold process. You must treat both yourself and others with grace, respect, and kindness. How you treat others, regardless if they are your lover, a family member, a friend, a co-worker or an adversary, communicating and acting in a caring manner is how you accomplish a mutually respectful relationship. The following do's and don'ts can apply to gain and maintain respect in all of your relationships.

- Avoid under-handed, back-stabbing, deceptive behavior.
- Never attack them personally or name-call during a heated discussion.
- Always speak in a calm tone of voice and avoid yelling or raising your voice.
- You can be firm and assertive without being abusive and aggressive.
- Listen and pay close attention to what they say.
- Respect their time, feelings, things, thoughts, and bodies
- Don't over ingratiate. Be sincere, honest, and genuine. People generally see right through over-indulgence and phoniness and lose respect for you.
- Be real and true to your convictions. Take a stand, express your opinions, even if they are unpopular. Substantiate your positions with factual and logical reasoning.
- You must give respect to get respect. Respect is earned. It is not automatic based on your position or title. You can have authority over someone at work or in your family but that doesn't mean your employees or children will automatically respect you.
- Don't confuse respect with people agreeing or disagreeing with you. If someone disagrees with you it doesn't necessarily mean that they don't respect you.

Integrity
Dictionary.Com offers 3 different definitions for the word *integrity*.

1. Adherence to moral and ethical principles; soundness of moral character; honesty
2. The state of being whole, entire, or undiminished: to preserve the integrity of the empire
3. A sound, unimpaired condition: the integrity of a ship's hull

When assessing a person's integrity all 3 of these definitions apply. Having integrity is an essential component in securing both others' respect and your self-respect. When you adhere to moral and ethical principles in a consistent manner you are on your way to gaining integrity. It doesn't necessarily have to be in agreement with everyone else's moral code but if you are consistent in verbalizing and behaving in a consistently moral manner your integrity will be intact. Following ethical principles established by organizations, the company you work for, and informal ethical rules in your social relationships creates moral character leading toward respect from others. Being honest and consistent in exhibiting moral character will help you gain social respect.

Referring to the second definition of integrity offered above, integrity is viewed as being whole and complete. It is used as a descriptive quality of the strength of an ideal. Your integrity must also be viewed as completeness, undiminished, and consistently strong. Differing from integrity as a consistent behavior set that you exhibit you must also convey integrity as part of who you are-your identity. People need to think of you as a person with integrity. That will occur if you consistently act with integrity.

The third and final definition offered has to do with strength. You must come across as a strong person. Don't confuse strength with power or authority. The type of strength that is associated with integrity has to do with being dependable, consistent, trustworthy, and reliable. So you can behave with integrity, be considered as a person with integrity, and you can have integrity as referred to inner strength and reliability. And remember the old adage, "the highest form of integrity is when you do the right thing even when no one is looking."

Morality

Morality has both universal and individual application with regard to having social respect. There are certain moral codes that apply to all people in terms of how to treat others, sexual contact, and a generally agreed upon rule system of social do's and don'ts when you are with other people. Some of the unwritten doctrine of moral behavior varies according to the nature of the relationship and situation. For example, it would be generally considered to be immoral to change into your bathing suit while you are at poolside. Displaying your body naked in front of strangers or friends would be considered to be inappropriate and immoral. However, changing into your bathing suit in the men's locker room (if you are a man) is considered to be moral and appropriate. When you greet your wife after work and put your hand on her buttocks when you kiss her is considered to be moral behavior. Can you imagine if you greeted your boss in this manner when you arrive at work in the morning?

Behaving in a moral manner facilitates social respect from others. Moral behavior equates to moral character, which is closely tied to integrity. It is your ability to follow the rules of society and interpersonal relationships. Social mores dictate right and wrong in terms of behavior. Adhering to those principles enables others to see you as a moral person. Despite the general moral conduct dictated by society, many individuals create their own moral principles that work for them within their relationship or mini-society. Morals should not be judged as inappropriate if they do not infringe upon the rights and feelings of others, and they are mutually consensual. Very early in my career I was having a session with a woman and we were discussing her sex life with her husband. She told me that her husband likes her to dress in slutty, very provocative clothing as part of their fore-play. She went on to describe how he is very domineering and controlling during love-making. I reflected what I thought she was feeling by saying, "That must make you feel uncomfortable and subordinate." The session ended but she called me the next day, upset with me. She referred to our discussion and how I made a judgment about how she felt regarding how her husband treated her during sex. I was trying to empathize with her and boost her self-esteem. She put me right in my place when she told me she really liked sex to be that way! I inappropriately imposed a moral code on the couple that did not apply to their specific situation.

Character

Your character is the core of who you are as an individual. Character envelopes your integrity and moral behavior. Character is something you own and are completely responsible for. Having character is a large part of having social respect. When people think about the kind of person you are, how you treat others, and what kind of human being you are, they are thinking about your character.

When people think of you as a person who has character, they view you as trustworthy and fair. Having character means that you are honest, you follow the rules, and are a loyal person to both ideals and others. Character gives you substance and depth, which are very attractive to most people. Caring about others is an inherent attribute usually associated with a person who has high moral character. Having character is not only about caring about others, but it is also caring about society, social issues, and generally being a good citizen and neighbor. If you are consistent in exhibiting all of these traits you are on your way to having a high degree of character and well-earned social respect. To solidify your quest for strong moral character you will need to go above and beyond in certain social interactions. It is the little things that go a long way to develop the consistent and stable perception that you are a person of high moral character. Some of those social actions include holding the door for people when entering a store or building, or helping them lift a heavy item into their shopping cart. Always displaying manners using "please" and "thank you" goes a long way. Going out of your way to let someone know that they have done a good job is always a pleasant surprise because people are so used to complaints and criticisms. I remember the first time my daughter had to take her care for servicing at the dealership. She was a young, new driver and was nervous because she wasn't sure where to go, what to tell them, and what to do. That evening I asked her how it went and she went on and on about how nice the service consultant was to her. Bob got her coffee while she waited, checked on her to see if she needed anything and explained everything that they were doing on her car. The next day I called the dealership and asked for Bob. When he got on the phone I explained to him that he serviced my daughter's car the day before. He immediately asked, "What is the problem?" I told him that I just wanted to thank him for treating my daughter so well and making her feel so comfortable in the service area. It was interesting that he immediately expected a complaint. Instead, he got a nicety. My kids make fun of me because I frequently write letters to customer service representatives and their bosses to let them know how wonderful their service was to me. It is these niceties that help give you character and subsequent social respect.

Self-Respect

Self-respect is yet another part of social respect. You cannot expect people to respect you if you do not respect yourself. Self-respect is evidenced initially by your physical appearance. Physical appearance is not equivalent to physical attractiveness. Physical appearance has to do with your personal hygiene and wearing appropriate attire for the specific social situation.

Having self-respect means treating yourself in a way that is caring and thoughtful. It is no different from respecting others in this sense. Self-respect encompasses all of the other traits associated with social respect. Self-respect is having integrity, morality, and character and applying it to yourself. Many people are extremely respectful of others and wouldn't dream of showing disrespect to peers or people in authority. But they lack respect for themselves and do not treat themselves as well as they treat others. In this case, the adage, "Do unto others as others would do unto you" becomes, "Do unto yourself as you do unto others."

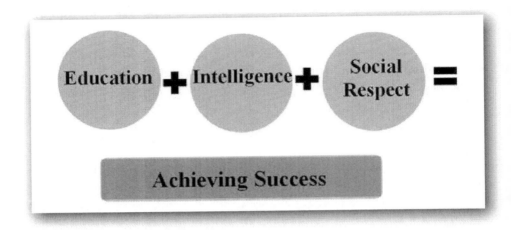

Achieving Success

Living a happy, free, self-fulfilled life is much easier to accomplish if you achieve success. The first thing you need to consider is what does success mean to you? For the purposes of this book, success is not defined by financial success. Success is the endpoint of living a life with the feeling and experience of being happy, free, and self-fulfilled. If you can accomplish this ultimate triad then you have achieved success in your life.

Success is not the endpoint but it can last for the duration of your life once you get to that place that you feel that you are living a successful life. Unfortunately, success can also be transient, elusive, and slippery. You can think you have success but there may be one or more aspects of your definition of success that you discover are not realized. Success is also a fluid concept because your definition of success may change or shift as you grow and develop. So, feeling you are living a successful life at 35-years-old may have a different definition when you reach 45-years-old. Success, like most of the triads in this book, needs to be constantly re-evaluated and adjusted.

Regardless of how you define success, or how that definition changes throughout your life, educating yourself, using the intelligence you were born with, and conducting your life in a manner that gives you social respect will significantly increase your potential to achieve it. Having knowledge, using logical, analytical, common sense thinking, and exhibiting integrity, moral be-havior, and character puts you in a place to attain your personal, social, and career goals.

Success can be self-perpetuating if you use it the right way. Using suc-cess successfully means that you are continuing to self-evaluate and constantly making adjustments when you see something in your life emerging with po-tential downfall. The following two examples illustrate a case study of some-one who made appropriate adjustments to maintain success and a case study of someone who did not.

Sanford-Living The Life

Sanford owned his own retail store and for years, enjoyed financial success and a happy family life. It was a well-established business, familiar to the neighbor-hood because it was originally opened by his father. He had good health, a good marriage, 2 young children, and an active social life. He appreciated and enjoyed living a successful life. At one point in time he began to notice that the neighborhood where his store was located began to deteriorate in terms of stability and crime. The buildings became run-down and drug use was in-creasing. It not only affected the traffic flow into his store, it began to deter his usual customers from coming in. Sanford, in his attempt to improve his slowly declining income, started working more hours to cut his labor overhead and to figure out ways to bring it back to where it had been. The increase in hours and stress began to have an impact on his home life and social life. Sanford quickly realized where this was going for him and decided that he needed to make a change.

Struggling with issues of legacy and longevity in his once friendly neigh-borhood store image, Sanford decided to relocate the store in a different part of town where the neighborhood replicated the old neighborhood. He strived to return to the balanced, successful life he had when the store flourished. It took some time, but once he moved the store, his formula for leading a suc-cessful life once again returned.

Connor-Stuck In His Ways

Connor's story also has his business as the focal point of determining his success, as well as his social life. Connor owned a printing shop, enjoyed financial success, and had been happily married for 4 years. He had no children, nor did he and his wife want to have children. The couple traveled a lot, enjoyed expensive hobbies both together and separately, and had an active social life. Two emerging changes began to occur around them. The couples with whom they enjoyed socializing with began to start having children. This created both a different head set and practical barriers in going out and vacationing with them. Those relationships slowly began to dwindle. The printing business also began to change. The amount of corporate accounts gradually began to decrease as companies realized that it was less expensive to create their own in-house printing services. Also, with the advent of the digital world, the need for printed and paper materials began to diminish.

Connor and his wife made no attempt to meet other couples their age, with no children, to socialize with. Connor made no attempt to change with the times, examining the new digital landscape of the printing world. He did not change his business model to adapt to the technology changes responsible for significantly decreasing his income. This had a ripple effect on the ability for Connor and his wife to travel and pursue costly hobbies. His failure to examine and adjust to the changing events in his life both socially and professionally began to impede his success and happiness.

CHAPTER 14

Quality Of Life

Keeping It Simple*Increasing Intensity*Letting It Go

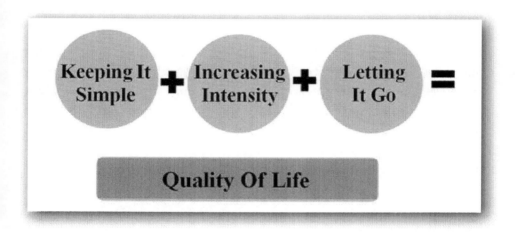

Keeping It Simple

There is something to be said for simplifying your life. The idea of having simplicity in your life means having a less complicated lifestyle. In this sense, simple is the opposite of complex. When things are uncomplicated there is less that can go wrong. At one time, decades ago, automobiles were sold with standard features such as a manual transmission, AM radio, and 2 speed windshield wipers. Today, cars are typically equipped with a multi-functional radio (AM, FM, Satellite), a CD player, Video player, air conditioning, heated seat, vented seats, power steering, power seat adjustments, electric mirrors, navigation systems, memory seats, cameras for blind spots and driving in reverse, multiple computer chips regulating both engine and comfort functions, automatic breaking, automatic parallel parking, keyless entry, keyless ignition and more. When cars were simpler, there was far less that could break. Today, despite the great benefits and convenience of how fully cars are equipped, there is a lot more that can go wrong.

Running your life so that the train does not leave without you sometimes means making your life simpler. With fewer complications, the potential for things going awry reduces. Charles Dudley Warner said, "Simplicity is making the journey of this life with just baggage enough." In other words, keep what is only necessary in your life to be happy. In American society there is a great deal of excess. We possess an excess in the amount of material objects. There is also an excess in the features attached to those material objects. In my book, *Generation Text: Raising Well Adjusted Kids In An Age Of Instant Everything* (Amacom, 2008) I give an example of almost 2 dozen different types of orange juice available in the supermarket. Again, options are great and are important to happiness, freedom, and self-fulfillment, but how many different types of OJ do we really need? How many varieties of OJ do we need to satisfy our orange juice enjoyment? Lester is an example of making a conscious decision to simplify his life.

Lester (Age 52)

Lester, married with 2 children, was becoming very overwhelmed and stressed on a daily basis. He owned a small accounting firm and was financially successful by most standards. In addition to his own home, he owned a small ski house in Vermont and a house down at the shore that he inherited from his parents. As we discussed the source of his overwhelmed and stressed feelings it became apparent that Lester was just doing too much. The demands of his life, as positive as they were, included his busy accounting practice, time attending to the needs of the ski and summer homes, and typical family demands. Even though his business, homes, and family were positive quality of life factors, all of these things were affecting the overall quality of his life in a negative way.

As we analyzed his role in his business and the actual use of the recreational homes, it rapidly became clear to Lester that he needed to simplify his life. Starting with his business, we started distributing some of his responsibilities to other employees. For example, instead of trying to manage his own schedule, he had his secretary/receptionist start scheduling his appointments. He began divvying up some of the menial tasks such as copying, mailing, and even payroll to capable employees.

Lester also decided that the ski and shore houses were receiving very limited use in recent years by his family due to the changes in his children's ages. Both, now in high school, were involved with sports and had active social lives. That made spending family time skiing and beaching very difficult due to practice schedules and decreased interest. His wife no longer enjoyed skiing and one of his children had a sun sensitive skin allergy. Consequently, he decided to sell both houses and simply rent for a week or weekend if they wanted to go skiing or down to the shore. By simplifying his life, Lester was able to significantly reduce the amount of demands and stress in his life.

Simplifying Your Life

Once again, I am asking you to step outside of yourself and look at your life from as an objective point of view as possible. What aspects, or people, in your life are complicating things for you? What can you eliminate to simplify your life so that there are less, demands or fewer things that can go wrong?

It doesn't always have to be a mammoth undertaking that simplifies your life. If you walk into a room in your house that is extremely cluttered, it makes it difficult to find something that you know is there. If everything is labeled, in boxes, shelved, and in a proper place, you can easily navigate through the objects to find what you need. Also, if you throw out what you really do not need in that room there will be less to sift through to find what you need. Is there "clutter" in your life? Do you have things or relationships that make your life complicated and more difficult? Do you engage in activities that cause more heartache for you, or preclude you from doing other things-even relaxing doing nothing at home? These are the types of things, people, and activities you need to eliminate in order to simplify your life.

There is another type of "clutter" to eliminate in your life. I call it emotional clutter. Emotional clutter are feelings associated with things and people that create feelings of frustration, anger, upset, depression, and inadequacy. I had a patient who played in a weekly tennis game with his friends. They played doubles and had 6 players rotating weekly so that 2 players would end up sitting out each week. My patient was, by his account, by far the worst player of the 6 players. They were all his friends so no one ever gave him a hard time about his sloppy play, but it was clear to my patient that he was disrupting the game due to his comparatively lower level of play. He began to feel upset, frustrated when it was his turn to play, and relieved when it was his week to sit out. On top of his emerging negative feelings about playing, he had other evening obligations with his children making it more cumbersome to go out yet another night after work. He began accumulating a great deal of emotional clutter until he realized that he should do something to simplify his life. He thought of quitting the tennis game but he still enjoyed the social aspect of it. Instead, he told his friends that due to his busy schedule he would have to become an alternate, playing only when they didn't have a fourth for doubles.

Wherever you can, try to simplify your life. Sometimes choosing what you can eliminate is very easy. Other times it may be confusing or difficult. Here is where you can employ the methods of cost-benefit and assessing the amount of risk discussed in Chapter 12.

Increasing Intensity

There are times in your life that it is important to increase the intensity of activities or relationships. It seems like I am now talking out of both sides of my mouth because increasing the intensity in your life is tantamount to adding something or increasing your involvement in existing activities and relationships. By doing so, it will usually make your life more complicated. Sometimes, it is better to step it up because life can become passive, boring, sedentary, and stifling if you keep it too simple for too long.

Intensity has a lot to do with increased emotions. When you bring anything up a notch in your life it will most likely result in an intensity of feelings. For example, if you are dating someone for 3 years and living together for 1 year, increasing the intensity might be to propose marriage to her. You can go on living together in a committed relationship, but making the relationship more formal and official would certainly increase the intensity. Asking your boss for a raise, looking for a higher paying job, or taking on more responsibility at work will all increase the intensity in your life. You can easily see how by increasing your intensity you will expand your universe, usually in a positive way. However, when you increase your intensity you also raise the risk for negative consequences. That should not deter you from increasing the intensity once you have made your due diligence in assessing the cost-benefit and risks in that particular situation.

By increasing your intensity, you can avoid feeling like your life is in a rut. If you do the same things with the same people all the time, life can become hum drum and boring. Remember it is safe to maintain the status quo, but there is a time and place to leave your comfort zone. Increasing your intensity is a necessary dimension to living a happy, free, and self-fulfilled life. People who do not increase their intensity from time to time usually make the train- but it is the same train all the time. Once in a while you need to make a different train.

Increasing your intensity promotes self-growth, pushes yourself outside of your comfort zone when you need to do so, and challenges yourself to new heights in your career, hobbies, and relationships. Let's look at a somewhat silly example using food.

The Same Ole Thing

I had a couple in marital therapy who went to the same restaurant every Friday night. They sat at the same table, had the same waiter, and ordered the same thing every time they visited this neighborhood grille. This routine kept them in their comfort zone but it also prevented them from experiencing different restaurants in the neighborhood, different foods, and different people. They started getting a bit bored with their routine so the wife suggested changing the restaurant. This increased the intensity because of the novelty of a new restaurant. They found their conversation to be different at dinner that night. There was a different feeling, a more excited feeling, a heightened sense of emotion. Now, this would not be an earth shattering, life altering experience for you or me, but it was for them. You can only imagine what it would be like for them if they increased the intensity they experience during lovemaking by altering their routine sex life!

Letting It Go

Similar to leaving it discussed in the previous chapter, letting it go means eliminating things in your life that do not serve you well. The difference is that leaving it is done after you are unable to solve a problem or stressful situation. Letting it go applies to routines, activities, and people in your life. The tennis player mentioned earlier, decided to let it go after he realized that playing tennis with his friends did not make him feel good and was no longer a fun activity. Lester, the accountant with 3 homes decided to let it go with certain responsibilities at work, as well as letting go of his 2 vacation homes.

When things, activities, and people no longer contribute to your life in a positive way you have two choices. You can either try to make changes or modifications so that the situation improves, or you can decide to simply let it go. Letting it go is usually difficult because most often the things you decide to finally let go of have been in your life for some time. This represents a significant change in your life. Consequently, letting it go can increase the intensity in your life in a negative emotional way. This will only be temporary because if you are letting something negative go it is for a good reason. Eventually, letting it go will improve some aspect of your life to create a good feeling. It is like getting an immunization. The shot may be fleetingly painful and there may be temporary side effects but in the end you are kept healthy. Sometimes you must go through a modicum of pain to get the gain. Letting it go can do that to you sometimes.

What To Let Go

What can you let go in your life? What activities don't you need to engage in any longer? Who do you let go of that you no longer derive pleasure from having a relationship with? Letting these things go means detaching yourself. Sometimes that requires an overt action and sometimes it means letting it go over time with the intention of eliminating it completely. If you want to break up with the guy you have been seeing for 6 months you let him know that you are letting him go. You make it clear, hopefully in a kind, caring way, that you no longer want to date him. You need to initiate an overt communication to let him know. But, if you want to phase out a friendship you probably want to give her the "slow no." Stop initiating getting together, decline her invitations, stop texting and responding to her social media posts. Eventually, she will move on and the friendship will phase out. The point is that if a relationship no longer serves you well for a variety of reasons it is appropriate to let it go.

You will need to let go of things as well as people at different times in your life. I love ice cream. I used to have ice cream every night after dinner. Fortunately, I keep fit by exercising and I have a generally healthy diet. At some point in my life I decided that I needed to let ice cream go because my metabolism was changing with age. That made it no longer healthy to have ice cream. I had to let it go. Okay, I do have ice cream once in a while-but only once in a while.

Letting Go Of Issues

There is another type of letting it go besides eliminating things, activities, and people in your life. It is letting go of an issue or a conflict you are having either with yourself or with another person. Letting go of an issue requires a combination of self-respect, self-confidence, self-righteousness, and forgiveness. It may also mean taking the high road and not making an issue over something not worth battling over. Some issues are just not worth the time and emotion to hold onto. I saw a presentation once and the lecturer held up a glass that was half full. He said, "I'm not going to do the half empty-half full philosophy. I want you to tell me if you think this glass is heavy or not." The audience responded with the obvious-that the 8-ounce glass half filled with water was not heavy at all. Then he asked, "What if I held this half-filled glass up just like this for 5 straight minutes? How heavy would it feel then? How about for one hour? Four hours, just like this in the same position? How about if I hold if for one day? One week? One year? Five years?" The point is that when something isn't that heavy, or important it can become a burdensome weight when you hold onto it for a long time. Holding onto issues and feelings for a long time can weigh you down considerably. That is when it is time to let it go.

Letting go of a conflict is indicated when the relationship is too important to you to hold onto a grudge. Whether you are right or wrong becomes unimportant. For the good of the relationship and to maintain your happiness, you let go of your position and subsequently, your feelings associated with it. Save your arguments for the really important issues and let go of the smaller ones. It may be difficult to distinguish between the small things you should let go and the important things you should keep filed away or continue to address. This is where your perspective comes into play, once again.

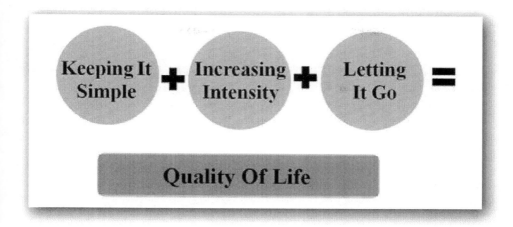

Quality Of Life

It is obvious that your overall quality of life has a direct connection to your happiness, freedom, and self-fulfillment. Quality of life is largely dependent on when you purposely keep things simple, when you increase your intensity, and when it is time to let something go. Like every triad in every chapter of this book, it requires a balance of all three dimensions. If you keep things overly simplified in your life, things could become one big routine and boring quite quickly. If you are forever increasing your intensity, your life will be manic, hectic, probably chaotic, and fraught with stress. If you let too many things go you will find yourself being taken advantage of, resentful, and angry. Balancing all three and knowing when to keep it simple, when to increase intensity, and when to let things go will help you lead a high quality of life.

Knowing which dimension to use and when to use it can be a very personal decision. That makes it quite difficult to outline a map to help you decide when to keep it simple, when to increase intensity, and when to let it go. To make matters a bit more complicated, it is not only when to use them, but it is in which situations and with whom do you use them. You will need to gauge both your feelings and a rational, logical thought process to help you decide. Learn what your triggers are for certain feelings. If you are feeling generally anxious, take a look at what is happening in the different aspects of your life to decide what changes you need to make. Maybe you need to simplify your life, or let something go. It is unlikely that you need to increase your intensity if you feel anxious. Feeling generally angry or irritable may be the trigger that signals that it may be time to make a change in a relationship or job. If you feel bored, it is time to increase the intensity in some area of your life. Do something different, do something novel, or do something exciting. Step outside your box and elevate your excitement. Cheri illustrates how she utilizes keeping it simple, increasing intensity, and letting it go with her 3 children. Notice how she carefully implements each dimension of the triad according to the situation, the individual child, and her timing.

Cheri

Cheri is a 44-year-old divorced mother of 3 children, ages 14, 12, and 7. Her ex-husband is only peripherally involved in terms of time, attention, and financial support of the children. He is an active alcoholic, is very unreliable, and at times, emotionally unstable. Cheri works 2 part-time jobs, manages the kids' schedules, chauffeurs them to school and their activities, and has the financial responsibility on her shoulders to keep the family's head above water. Her 14-year-old son is old enough and responsible enough to watch his younger brother and sister but that is only so that Cheri can run errands and manage her work schedule. She has very little time for herself as she spends the majority of her waking hours managing the family's needs. Her parents and sister live in another state so there is not a family support system nearby to help her out. She has had to hire a college student to do some driving so that the kids could get to their activities. As this scenario trudged on for several years, Cheri began to feel exhausted, stressed, and unhappy most of the time. She took a look at her life and how it was panning out and did not like what she saw. She decided that it was time to make some changes. Cheri began to employ the three dimensions of keeping it simple, increasing intensity, and letting it go in order to improve her overall quality of life.

First, to simplify her life, she realized that working two part-time jobs in two separate medical practices created extra time commuting and less flexibility with her free and family time. She realized that working one full-time job would eliminate the extra traveling time, would reduce the cost of commuting, create less juggling to attend her children's events, and could increase her benefits and salary. So, to simplify her life, Cheri secured a full-time position with higher pay in an office that was even closer to her home. It created less stress for her, gave her a semblance of more control in her life, and made it easier to free her up to attend school and athletic functions. The benefit of the extra salary was somewhat compromised because she had to rely a bit more on her college student chauffeur/babysitter but simplifying her life made it worth it.

After the re-evaluation of her life, the second thing Cheri decided to do was increase her intensity. Her children were getting older and becoming increasingly more independent. She realized that it was time to attend to her own needs more than she had been in recent years. It was time to put herself out there and start dating. She recently met a man she often ran into at the Starbucks on her way to her new job every morning. They ran into each other most mornings and began an "on line" relationship. This was literally, an "on line" relationship, not an "online" relationship. Waiting their turn to order their morning coffee, they met on line and talked on the line. That was the extent of their relationship but she found herself attracted to him and sensed he felt the same way. She put the right signals out and he perceptively picked them up and they started seeing each other.

Addressing the "letting it go" piece of the triad to improve her quality of life involved a conscious decision regarding her ex-husband. Cheri decided that she had to let go of the anger and resentment she was holding onto due to his alcohol use and the unreliable, emotionally volatile behaviors associated with it. She was legally divorced and now she had to divorce herself of the turmoil he created with anyone he interacted with. She changed her expectations for him as the father of their children and as a financial support to them. Her frequent disappointment when he didn't show up for his parenting time, was late arriving, or not having the money to pay for incidentals such as the Pop Warner Football fee or outfit for the dance recital were no longer going to upset her because she just wouldn't expect it of him in the first place. Letting go of her anger, resentment, and expectations would certainly help improve her quality of life.

CHAPTER 15

Be Happy, Free, And Self-Fulfilled

Using The Triads

Admittedly, I gave you a lot to do and a lot to think about. I realize it isn't simple and easy. Happiness, freedom, and self-fulfillment is a physical and emotional state of being that requires constant work, adjusting, modifying and changing. As you develop, your internal world changes resulting in changes in what you need to be happy. As you go through your life, your environmental situations and relationship constantly change, also necessitating modifications in how you are navigating through the triads. It would be great if you are already working on or are implementing some of the triads presented. Many of them are simply common sense and logical. Even if you found some of the ideas to be elementary and basic, it is always good to revisit them to reinforce their presence in your life. Hopefully, there were many ideas presented that you haven't yet thought of applying to yourself.

Using the triads as tools to guide your life will enhance your happiness, increase your freedom, and help you attain self-fulfillment. This should not be a book that you shelve after you read it, or just keep stored in your electronic device's cache. It should be referenced with some frequency as a reminder to keep you on track. The components in each triad that produce each important life function should be periodically assessed and reassessed. Many circumstances and issues in life wax and wane and none of these circles are immune to slowly weakening or drifting away without you realizing it. Stepping outside of yourself and trying to be as objective as possible is a great way to uncover a weakening circle. When you identify a weak circle you will need to attend to it to bolster its strength again. This entails making either minor or major adjustments to the status quo. By doing so, you will prevent it from going too far making it more insurmountable to correct. The faster you attend to a weakening circle the easier it will be to set it on course again.

Balance, Balance, Balance

The roadmap presented for a happy, free, and self-fulfilled life includes mastery over the following functions.

- Freedom
- Relationships
- Selfishless
- Identity
- Work Ethic
- Problem Solving
- Coping With Stress
- Competence
- Comfort Zone
- Achieving Success
- Quality of Life

As you may have realized, each of these life functions are contingent upon balancing all 3 components. Within each life function, the components are independent from one another, yet they are not mutually exclusive due to the need for a homeostatic relationship among them. Too much or too little of one circle taints the whole picture and makes it more difficult to attain success. For example, your work ethic will be negatively affected if you work hard at what you do, are organized, but rush through it because you don't work toward excellence. Similarly, if you are caring and respectful in your relationships but are not honest, you will not have healthy relationships.

It is not an accident that there are many references to other chapters within the text. Just as the components within a life function are interrelated, the life functions are also interrelated. For example, the quality of your relationships is highly contingent upon the successful fulfillment of all of the other life functions. Individual attention to each and every one of the life functions is important and they are separate, but not mutually exclusive. Not one of the life functions could be considered to be the most important. They are all important. They all require your addressing each component and strengthening the weak circle. Many of them can be accomplished with a certain degree of success even if one circle is slightly weaker. The exception would be the life function of relationships. Relationships cannot be successful and healthy if they are not strong in honesty, love/care, and respect. Work ethic can be considered a crucial life function because if you have a great work ethic, you can apply it to a successful effort in meeting the needs of all of the other life functions. They all enhance and complement each other in many ways. They build upon each other. For example, if you use effective coping strategies you will have a good perspective on problem solving. Having a secure *identity* a balanced *comfort zone*, balance in your *giving,* and a strong sense of *competence* will greatly enhance the quality and healthiness of your *relationships.* If you attend to all of the life functions, it is almost a guarantee that you will live a life filled with happiness, freedom, and self-fulfillment.

One of the most important factors in evaluating a great property in real estate is *location, location, location.* One of the most important factors in seeking a happy, free, and self-fulfilled life is *balance, balance, balance.* Balance is not only required within each triad, but overall balance is necessary between all of the life functions presented. If your work ethic is so strong and you spend too much time working, it may affect the quality of your relationships. Achieving success will be highly contingent upon a balance between problem solving, coping with stress, and handling your comfort zone. Your overall quality of life depends on a balance among all of these life functions. I encourage you to try to mend and maintain these triads as best as you can. Handling them independently is empowering and rewarding. But, realize that it may be necessary from time to time to seek the help of professionals to enhance or repair your life. If your car is making a funny noise you might try to figure out what the problem is on your own. But if you can't, you wouldn't think twice about bringing it in to a mechanic. Why wouldn't you fix yourself the same way?

Always remember that you are entitled to, and deserve to have a happy, free, and self-fulfilled life. By entitled, I don't mean that it doesn't have to be earned. By addressing all of these self needs in balance with the demands of your social environment, and coping with the problems and stresses that will undoubtedly occur, you will greatly increase the chance of living happy. Even if you do all of these things excellently, don't be naïve to think that the train will never leave without you. But, you will make that train most of the time, enjoy the ride, and enjoy yourself when you get to your destination.

Made in the USA
Middletown, DE
30 October 2016